**2011 EDITION**

# campsites

## for **fishing**

alan
rogers

Compiled by: Alan Rogers Guides Ltd

Designed by: Vine Design Ltd

© Alan Rogers Guides Ltd 2010

Published by: Alan Rogers Guides Ltd,
Spelmonden Old Oast, Goudhurst, Kent TN17 1HE
www.alanrogers.com
Tel: 01580 214000

British Library Cataloguing-in-Publication Data:
A catalogue record for this book is available from
the British Library.

ISBN 978-1-906215-37-8

Printed in Great Britain by
Stephens & George Print Group

# contents

# Welcome to the Alan Rogers
# '101' **guides**

The Alan Rogers guides have been helping campers and caravanners make informed decisions about their holiday destinations since 1968. Today, whether online or in print, Alan Rogers still provides an independent, impartial view, with detailed reports, on each campsite.

With so much unfiltered, unqualified information freely available, the Alan Rogers perspective is invaluable to make sure you make the right choice for your holiday.

## What is the '101' **series**?

At Alan Rogers, we know that readers have many and diverse interests, hobbies and particular requirements. And we know that our guides, featuring a total of some 3,000 campsites, can provide a bewildering choice from which it can be difficult to produce a shortlist of possible holiday destinations.

The Alan Rogers 101 guides are devised as a means of presenting a realistic, digestible number of great campsites, featured because of their suitability to a given theme.

This book remains first and foremost an authoritative guide to excellent campsites which offer great holidays for fishing enthusiasts.

## 101 **Best campsites for fishing**

Fishing is perhaps one of the most popular pastimes on campsites across Europe. Campsites being mostly rural, water is often close by or on site in the form of rivers, lakes, ponds, streams or the sea. So whether you enjoy coarse fishing, sea fishing or fly fishing, there are campsites that can oblige.

Some campsites have developed their fishing facilities with purpose-built lakes, waterside accommodation, equipment hire and the like. Others simply find themselves well-placed geographically and geologically – maybe close to the sea or to a great trout stream.

This guide features campsites that consider themselves great destinations for fishing.

They may offer elaborate facilities for serious anglers looking for 'the big one' or they may just cater for enthusiastic fishermen (and children) just wanting to try their luck.

Whether you are an angling expert, or a parent keen to find a great campsite with good fishing facilities for the kids this summer, read on. There are 101 campsites in this guide and, depending on what kind of fishing you're looking for, and at what level, you are sure to find your ideal holiday destination here.

# Alan Rogers – in search
# of 'the best'

Alan Rogers himself started off with the very specific aim of providing people with the necessary information to allow them to make an informed decision about their holiday destination. Today we still do that with a range of guides that now covers Europe's best campsites in 27 countries.

We work with campsites all day, every day. We visit campsites for inspection purposes (or even just for pleasure!). We know campsites 'inside out'.

We know which campsites would suit active families; which are great for get-away-from-it-all couples; we know which campsites are planning super new pool complexes; which campsites offer a fantastic menu in their on-site restaurant; which campsites allow you to launch a small boat from their slipway; which campsites have a decent playing area for kicking a ball around; which campsites have flat, grassy pitches and which have solid hard standings.

We also know which are good for fishing, golf, spas and outdoor activities; which are close to the beach; and which welcome dogs. These particular themes form our new '101' series.

All Alan Rogers guides (and our website) are respected for their independent, impartial and honest assessment. The reviews are prose-based, without overuse of indecipherable icons and symbols. Our simple aim is to help guide you to a campsite that matches best your requirements – often quite difficult in today's age of information overload.

## What is the **best**?

The criteria we use when inspecting and selecting sites are numerous, but the most important by far is the question of good quality. People want different things from their choice of campsite, so campsite 'styles' vary dramatically: from small peaceful campsites in the heart of the countryside, to 'all singing, all dancing' sites in popular seaside resorts.

The size of the site, whether it's part of a chain or privately owned, makes no difference in terms of it being required to meet our exacting standards in respect of its quality and it being 'fit for purpose'. In other words, irrespective of the size of the site, or the number of facilities it offers, we consider and evaluate the welcome, the pitches, the sanitary facilities, the cleanliness, the general maintenance and even the location.

## **Expert** opinions

We rely on our dedicated team of Site Assessors, all of whom are experienced campers, caravanners or motorcaravanners, to visit and recommend campsites. Each year they travel around Europe inspecting new campsites for Alan Rogers and re-inspecting the existing ones.

# When planning your **holiday...**

A holiday should always be a relaxing affair, and a campsite-based holiday particularly so. Our aim is for you to find the ideal campsite for your holiday, one that suits your requirements. All Alan Rogers guides provide a wealth of information, including some details supplied by campsite owners themselves, and the following points may help ensure that you plan a successful holiday.

## Find out more

An Alan Rogers reference number (**e.g. FR12345**) is given for each campsite and can be useful for finding more information and pictures online at **www.alanrogers.com**

Simply enter this number in the 'Campsite Search' field on the Home page.

## Campsite descriptions

We aim to convey an idea of its general appearance, 'feel' and features, with details of pitch numbers, electricity, hardstandings etc.

## Facilities

We list specific information on the site's facilities and amenities and, where available, the dates when these facilities are open (if not for the whole season). Much of this information is as supplied to us and may be subject to change. Should any particular activity or aspect of the campsite be important to you, it is always worth discussing with the campsite before you travel.

## Swimming pools

Opening dates, any charges and levels of supervision are provided where we have been notified. In some countries (notably France) there is a regulation whereby Bermuda-style shorts may not be worn in swimming pools (for health and hygiene reasons). It is worth ensuring that you do take 'proper' swimming trunks with you.

### Charges

Those given are the latest provided to us, usually 2010 prices, and should be viewed as a guide only.

### Toilet blocks

We assume that toilet blocks will be equipped with a reasonable number of British style WCs, washbasins and hot showers in cubicles. We also assume that there will be an identified chemical toilet disposal point, and that the campsite will provide water and waste water drainage points and bin areas. If not the case, we comment. We do mention certain features that some readers find important: washbasins in cubicles, facilities for babies, facilities for those with disabilities and motorcaravan service points.

### Reservations

Necessary for high season (roughly mid-July to mid-August) in popular holiday areas (i.e. beach resorts). You can reserve many sites via our own Alan Rogers Travel Service or through other tour operators. Remember, many sites are closed all winter and you may struggle to get an answer.

### Telephone numbers

All numbers assume that you are phoning from within the country in question. From the UK or Ireland, dial 00, then the country's prefix (e.g. France is 33), then the campsite number given, but dropping the first '0'.

### Opening dates

Dates given are those provided to us and can alter before the start of the season. If you intend to visit shortly after a published opening date, or shortly before the closing date, it is wise to check that it will actually be open at the time required. Similarly, some sites operate a restricted service during the low season, only opening some of their facilities (e.g. swimming pools) during the main season; where we know about this, and have the relevant dates, we indicate it – again if you are at all doubtful it is wise to check.

### Accommodation

Over recent years, more and more campsites have added high quality mobile homes, chalets, lodges, gites and more. Where applicable we indicate what is available and you'll find details online.

### Special Offers

Some campsites have taken the opportunity to highlight a special offer. This is arranged by them and for clarification please contact the campsite direct.

# Fishing
# for **all**

A camping holiday is a great chance to indulge in a spot of fishing. It's an ideal scenario, a happy combination of (hopefully) sunny weather, fresh air, pleasant scenery and a convenient location not far from good fishing spots. So, whatever kind of fishing you fancy, and at whatever level, take this guide as a starting point for planning your fishing holiday.

# Choosing campsites for fishing

This guide sets out to identify great campsites which offer excellent fishing opportunities. With over 4 million anglers to consider in the UK alone, some sites have well developed fishing facilities, with purpose-built lakes, equipment hire and features geared for the serious angler. Some, such as Cofton Country Holidays in the West Country, even have on-site accommodation close to the water's edge with anglers in mind. Of course, if you have highly specific requirements, and plan some competitive fishing, you should check all details before you commit.

Other campsites appeal to fishing fans by virtue of their location: perhaps close to great beach fishing spots or sea fishing hire boats, or adjacent to long stretches of river.

# Fishing,
# your **way**

## **Sea** fishing

The coast provides endless opportunities for sea anglers, with many species of fish available all year and for free!

### Shore fishing

Piers and jetties are ideal places for catching mackerel, while mullet, flounder and dab frequent estuaries and harbours. The foam covered seas next to rocky headlands are home to wrasse and conger eel, and beaches offer the chance to catch bass, whiting and ray.

### Boat fishing

Most seaside resorts offer fishing trips, a chance to spend a half day or so experiencing the thrill of sea fishing. Rods and bait are usually provided and the skipper of the boat will try to ensure that fish are caught.

## **Coarse** fishing

Coarse fishing encompasses any freshwater fish, other than salmon or trout which are considered game fish. These include roach, perch, tench, carp, bream, rudd, pike and chub, to name but a few. There are many types of coarse angler, ranging from the pleasure angler, through the match angler to the specialist anglers and specimen hunters.

## **Fly** fishing

Fly fishing is associated with trout and salmon, though many other fish may be caught this way. It offers a more stripped-down 'man against nature' experience coupled with evocative images of standing waist-deep in fast running waters amid beautiful scenery.

With fly fishing the weight of the line propels the cast, not the weight of the bait or lure. A fly may be very light but, with a graceful and experienced flick, it can be presented to a fish 40 feet away.

## Getting **started**

Tackle can be the source of endless debate. For some, fishing boils down to sticking a worm on a hook; for others 'bait presentation' is a dark art. Either way, for fishing at a basic level, you will need the following:

- Decent all round fishing rod
  *(around 10 to 12 feet in length)*

- Robust fixed-spool reel

- 100-200 metres of line
  *(about 4-5lb breaking strain)*

- Selection of hooks, sizes 18-12

- Selection of floats

- Split-shot dispenser

- Rod rests

- Stool or chair

- Selection of bait

- Landing net

- Licence

## Fishing **Licences**

There are exceptions, but usually you need a licence to fish, unless actually fishing in a lake or pond on-site. Campsite reception, or the fishing shop, will advise you on where to obtain a licence (often the post office or local shop). You may need to provide a passport by way of ID. Children under a certain age don't always need a licence, but they might well need to be accompanied by an older angler with a fishing licence.

# Getting hooked
# on **fishing**

## **Top** tips

Every fishing situation is different but a few tips to get you on your way…. (we know all anglers love tips!).

- Keep a low profile – avoid shadows and silhouettes on the water

- Silence is crucial – fish use their whole body to detect noise vibrations

- Overhanging branches and submerged features like trees are often good spots to start from

- Try and establish the depth of the water to enable you to fish at the correct depth

- When discarding old line, chop it up to ensure it doesn't cause suffering to wildlife

- Fancy tackle can catch more anglers than fish – unless you know exactly what you are doing, keep it simple!

- Small clouds of bubbles can indicate presence of grazing fish *(eg tench or bream)*

- Polarised sunglasses cut through reflections and glare on the water

- For night time fishing a head torch can be useful

- When beach angling, start a couple of hours before high tide – the rising water disturbs food species like shrimp and thus attracts fish in to feed

- Chat to other anglers and to campsite staff: there will be others around who can tell you about the best times, conditions and local tips.

## Fishing **for children**

And of course fishing for youngsters is an integral part of the holiday: neither competitive nor serious, simply a chance to enjoy the prospect of a catch, to interact with one's natural surroundings, to learn respect for animals and perhaps a little patience too.

The first fishing excursion is a popular step on from pond dipping, and other similar childhood 'moments' that are often wrapped in the warm glow of nostalgia. It's a perfect opportunity for adult and child to spend quality time together.

Keep these initial excursions fairly short, taking a picnic as well as binoculars (for spotting birds and other animals), a camera and a bag for collecting souvenir finds of feathers, leaves, animal fur and whatever else sparks the child's curiosity.

Find a spot where the fishing is gentle, like a pool or slow moving water, and keep things as simple as possible. Ideally choose somewhere frequented by minnows or shoals of fry where a catch is almost guaranteed.

## Enjoy...!

Whether you're an 'old hand' or are contemplating your first trip, a regular reader of our Guides or a new 'convert', we wish you well in your travels and hope we have been able to help in some way. We are, of course, also out and about ourselves, visiting sites, talking to owners and readers, and generally checking on standards and new developments. We hope to bump into you!

Wishing you thoroughly enjoyable camping and caravanning in 2011 – favoured by good weather of course!

The Alan Rogers Team

# And before
# you go...

## Some **basic rules**

Again, we can't legislate for every swim you'll come across but, for the relatively uninitiated, here are some common ground rules to be aware of.

- Beware of snagging bankside trees, vegetation and obstructions in the water
- Take care where people feed waterfowl
- Never leave rods unattended while fishing
- Never leave rods on the bank with hooks still baited, as these could be picked up by birds or animals
- Beware of birds swimming into your line or picking up surface baits
- Keep lines under the surface to avoid waterfowl
- Keep the environment clean and tidy up all your belongings

## Further **information**

www.pcfa.co.uk – *Professional Coarse Fisheries Association*
www.fisheries.co.uk – *Coarse fishing*

www.sea-fishing.org
www.worldseafishing.com

www.fishandfly.com
www.flyfishingforbeginners.com

www.environment-agency.gov.uk – *Buy a UK licence online*

### For Kids

www.fishing4fun.co.uk
www.ghof.org.uk

# Camping Roche

N340 km 19,5, Carril de Pilahito, E-11140 Conil de la Frontera (Cádiz)
t: 956 442 216  e: info@campingroche.com
alanrogers.com/ES88590  www.campingroche.com

Accommodation: ☑Pitch  ☑Mobile home/chalet  ☐Hotel/B&B  ☐Apartment

Camping Roche is situated in a pine forest near white sandy beaches in the lovely region of Andalucia. It is a clean and tidy, welcoming site. Little English is spoken but try your Spanish, German or French as the staff are very helpful. A family site, it offers a variety of facilities including a sports area and swimming pools. The restaurant has good food and a pleasant outlook over the pool. Games are organised for children. A recently built extension provides further pitches, a new toilet block and a tennis court. There are 335 pitches which include 104 bungalows to rent. There are pleasant paths in the area for mountain biking and this is an ideal base for visiting the cities of Seville and Cádiz.

## You might like to know
We recommend a visit to Conil de la Frontera, a delightful town wth its calas and ancient church.

☐ Coarse fishing
☐ Fly fishing
☑ Sea fishing
☐ Lake on site
☑ River on site
☐ Lake nearby (max 5 km)
☑ River nearby (max 5 km)
☐ Licence / permit required
☑ Equipment hire available
☑ Bait and fishing supplies

**Facilities:** Three toilet blocks are traditional in style and provide simple, clean facilities. Washbasins have cold water only. Washing machine. Supermarket. Bar and restaurant. Swimming and paddling pools. Sports area. Tennis. Play area. Off site: Bus stops 3 times daily outside gates.

**Open:** All year.

**Directions:** From the N340 (Cádiz - Algeciras) turn off to site at km. 19.5 point. From Conil, take El Pradillo road. Keep following signs to site. From CA3208 road turn at km. 1 and site is 1.5 km. down this road on the right. GPS: 36.31089, -6.11268

### Charges guide

| | |
|---|---|
| Per unit incl. 2 persons and electricity | € 33,00 |
| extra person | € 6,50 |
| child | € 5,50 |
| dog | € 3,75 |

Low season discounts.

# Camping Nautic Almata

Ctra. GIV- 6216 km 11,6, E-17486 Castelló d'Empúries (Girona)
t: **972 454 477**  e: **info@almata.com**
alanrogers.com/ES80300  www.almata.com

**Accommodation:** ☑Pitch ☑Mobile home/chalet ☐ Hotel/B&B ☐ Apartment

In the Bay of Roses, south of Empúriabrava and beside the Parc Natural dels Aiguamolls de l'Empordá, this is a high quality site of particular interest to nature lovers (especially bird watchers). Beautifully laid out, it is arranged around the river and waterways, so will suit those who like to be close to water or who enjoy watersports and boating. It is worth visiting because of its unusual aspects and the feeling of being on the canals, as well as being a superb beachside site. A large site, there are 1,109 well kept, large, numbered pitches, all with electricity and on flat, sandy ground. There are some pitches right on the beach and on the banks of the canal. As you drive through the natural park to the site, watch for the warning signs for frogs on the road and enjoy the wild flamingos alongside the road. The name no doubt derives from the fact that boats can be tied up at the small marina within the site and a slipway also gives access to a river and thence to the sea. Throughout the season there is a varied entertainment programme for children and adults. The facilities on this site are impressive.

## You might like to know

The adjacent nature park is made up of enclosed meadows, lagoons and irrigation channels lying between the Muga and the Fluvia rivers and forming a natural area brimming with flora and fauna.

- ☑ **Coarse fishing**
- ☐ Fly fishing
- ☑ **Sea fishing**
- ☐ Lake on site
- ☐ River on site
- ☑ **Lake nearby (max 5 km)**
- ☑ **River nearby (max 5 km)**
- ☑ **Licence / permit required**
- ☐ Equipment hire available
- ☐ Bait and fishing supplies

**Facilities:** Toilet blocks of a high standard include some en-suite showers with basins. Good facilities for disabled visitors. Washing machines. Gas supplies. Excellent supermarket. Restaurants and bar. Two separate bars and snack bar by beach where discos are held in main season. Water-skiing, diving and windsurfing schools. 300 m² swimming pool. New tennis court. Squash. Fronton. Minigolf. Games room. Extensive riding tuition with own stables and stud. New children's play park. Fishing (licence required). Car, motorcycle and bicycle hire. Hairdresser. Internet access and WiFi. ATM. Torches are useful near beach. Off site: Canal trips 18 km. Aquatic Park 20 km.

**Open:** 14 May - 18 September (with all services).

**Directions:** Site is signed at 26 km. marker on C252 between Castello d'Empúries and Vildemat, then 7 km. to site. Alternatively, on San Pescador - Castello d'Empuries road head north and site is well signed. GPS: 42.1245, 3.0510

## Charges guide

| | |
|---|---|
| Per unit incl. 1-6 persons | € 22,50 - € 45,00 |
| extra person (over 3 yrs) | € 2,50 - € 5,00 |
| dog | € 5,00 - € 6,60 |
| boat or jet ski | € 9,50 - € 12,50 |

No credit cards.

# Camping Picos de Europa

E-33556 Avin-Onis (Asturias)
t: **985 844 070**  e: **info@picos-europa.com**
alanrogers.com/ES89650  www.picos-europa.com

Accommodation: ☑Pitch ☑Mobile home/chalet ☐Hotel/B&B ☑Apartment

This delightful site is, as its name suggests, an ideal spot from which to explore these dramatic limestone mountains on foot, by bicycle or on horseback. The site itself is continuously developing and the dynamic owner, José, or his nephew who helps out when he is away, are both very pleasant and nothing is too much trouble. The site is in a valley beside a pleasant, fast flowing river. The 160 marked pitches are of varying sizes and have been developed in three avenues, on level grass mostly backing on to hedging, with 6A electricity. An area for tents and apartments is over a bridge past the fairly small, but pleasant, round swimming pool. Local stone has been used for the L-shaped building at the main entrance which houses reception and a very good bar/restaurant. The site can organise caving activities, and has information about the Cares gorge along with the many energetic ways of exploring the area, including by canoe and quad-bike! The Bulnes funicular railway is well worth a visit.

## You might like to know

Off site, why not try the Sella Descent, a white water rafting challenge in the river section between Arriondas and Ribadesella, using one, two or three seat kayaks and canoes.

- ☑ Coarse fishing
- ☐ Fly fishing
- ☐ Sea fishing
- ☐ Lake on site
- ☐ River on site
- ☐ Lake nearby (max 5 km)
- ☐ River nearby (max 5 km)
- ☑ Licence / permit required
- ☐ Equipment hire available
- ☐ Bait and fishing supplies

**Facilities:** Toilet facilities include a new fully equipped block, along with new facilities for disabled visitors and babies. Pleasant room with tables and chairs for poor weather. Washing machine and dryer. Shop (July-Sept). Swimming pool (Feb-Sept). Bar and cafeteria style restaurant (all year) serves a good value 'menu del dia' and snacks. WiFi in restaurant area. Play area. Fishing. Torches necessary in the new tent area. Off site: Riding 12 km. Bicycle hire 15 km. Golf 25 km. Coast at Llanes 25 km.

**Open:** All year.

**Directions:** Avin is 15 km. east of Cangas de Onis on AS114 road to Panes and is probably best approached from this direction especially if towing. From A8 (Santander - Oviedo) use km. 326 exit and N634 northwest to Arriondas. Turn southeast on N625 to Cangas and join AS114 (Covodonga/Panes) by-passing Cangas. Site is just beyond Avin after 16 km. marker. GPS: 43.3363, -4.94498

**Charges guide**

| | |
|---|---|
| Per person | € 5,02 |
| child (under 14 yrs) | € 4,01 |
| pitch incl. car | € 8,57 - € 9,64 |
| electricity | € 3,75 |

# Camping Playa Joyel

Playa de Ris, E-39180 Noja (Cantabria)
t: 942 630 081   e: playajoyel@telefonica.net
alanrogers.com/ES90000   www.playajoyel.com

**Accommodation:** ☑Pitch ☑Mobile home/chalet ☐ Hotel/B&B ☐ Apartment

This very attractive holiday and touring site is some 40 kilometres from Santander and 80 kilometres from Bilbao. It is a busy, high quality, comprehensively equipped site by a superb beach providing 1,000 well shaded, marked and numbered pitches with 6A electricity available. These include 80 large pitches of 100 m$^2$. Some 250 pitches are occupied by tour operators or seasonal units. This well managed site has a lot to offer for family holidays with much going on in high season when it gets crowded. The swimming pool complex (with lifeguard) is free to campers and the superb beaches are cleaned daily (15/6-20/9). Two beach exits lead to the main beach where there are some undertows, or if you turn left you will find a reasonably placid estuary. An unusual feature here is the nature park within the site boundary which has a selection of animals to see. This overlooks a protected area of marsh where European birds spend the winter.

## You might like to know

Playa Joyel is located on the Cantabrian Sea and surrounded by Noja Natural Wetlands Reserve and the beautiful extensive sandy beach of Ris. Opposite Ris is the island of San Pedruco, a natural paradise protected by an abundance of vegetation and inhabited by thousands of seagulls.

☑ Coarse fishing
☐ Fly fishing
☑ Sea fishing
☐ Lake on site
☐ River on site
☑ Lake nearby (max 5 km)
☐ River nearby (max 5 km)
☑ Licence / permit required
☐ Equipment hire available
☐ Bait and fishing supplies

**Facilities:** Six excellent, spacious and fully equipped toilet blocks include baby baths. Large laundry. Motorcaravan services. Gas supplies. Freezer service. Supermarket (all season). General shop. Kiosk. Restaurant and takeaway (1/7-31/8). Bar and snacks (all season). Swimming pools, caps compulsory (20/5-15/9). Entertainment organised with a soundproofed pub/disco (July/Aug). Gym park. Tennis. Playground. Riding. Fishing. Nature animal park. Hairdresser (July/Aug). Medical centre. Torches necessary in some areas. Animals are not accepted. Off site: Bicycle hire and large sports complex with multiple facilities including an indoor pool 1 km. Sailing and boat launching 10 km.

**Open:** 15 April - 1 October.

**Directions:** From A8 (Bilbao - Santander) take km. 185 exit and N634 towards Beranga. Almost immediately turn right on CA147 to Noja. In 10 km. turn left at multiple campsite signs and go through town. At beach follow signs to site. GPS: 43.48948, -3.53700

**Charges 2011**

| Per unit incl. 2 persons and electricity | € 28,20 - € 47,40 |
|---|---|
| extra person | € 4,40 - € 6,70 |
| child (3-9 yrs) | € 3,10 - € 5,00 |

# Camping de La Rioja

Ctra de Haro - Sto Domingo de la Calzada, E-26240 Castanares de Rioja (La Rioja)
t: 941 300 174   e: info@campingdelarioja.com
alanrogers.com/ES92250

Accommodation: ☑Pitch  ☑Mobile home/chalet  ☐Hotel/B&B  ☐Apartment

This site is situated just beyond the town of Castanares de Rioja. This is a busy site during the peak season with many sporting activities taking place. In low season it becomes rather more quiet with limited facilities available. There are 30 level, grass touring pitches, out of a total of 250, and these are separated by hedges and trees allowing privacy. Each has their own water, drainage and electricity connection. To the rear of the site is the Oja River which is ideal for fishing and there are views of the Obarenes mountains in the distance. Some noise from the main road is possible. There are many historic places worth visiting and naturally, being in Rioja, plenty of local wine to taste. A walk or cycle into the town of Castanares will enable you to sample the local cuisine.

## You might like to know
The Oja river flows through this attractive region and is widely believed to have given its name to the famous wine of the area, although there are other theories.

- ☑ Coarse fishing
- ☐ Fly fishing
- ☐ Sea fishing
- ☐ Lake on site
- ☑ River on site
- ☐ Lake nearby (max 5 km)
- ☐ River nearby (max 5 km)
- ☑ Licence / permit required
- ☐ Equipment hire available
- ☐ Bait and fishing supplies

**Facilities:** The central sanitary facilities are old and traditional in style but clean. Open style washbasins and controllable showers. Laundry and dishwashing facilities. Shop, bar, restaurant, takeaway (on request, all open 20/6-20/9). Outdoor swimming pool (20/6-20/9 supervised). Multisport court. Football. Tennis. River fishing. Riding. Children's cycle circuit. Play area. No individual barbecues. Off site: Town centre 1.5 km. The Guggenheim Museum in Bilbao. City of San Sebastian with beaches and aquarium.

**Open:** 1 January - 9 December.

**Directions:** Head west on N120. Turn right onto LR111 signed Castanares de Rioja. Continue through town towards Haro. Site is on left, 800 m. after leaving town speed restriction. GPS: 42.52911, -2.92243

**Charges guide**

| Per person | € 4,60 - € 5,75 |
| --- | --- |
| child | € 4,00 - € 5,00 |
| pitch | € 10,00 - € 12,50 |
| electricity | € 3,60 |

# Orbitur Camping Caminha

EN13 km 90, Mata do Camarido, P-4910-180 Caminha (Viana do Costelo)
t: 258 921 295  e: info@orbitur.pt
alanrogers.com/PO8010  www.orbitur.pt

**Accommodation:** ☑ Pitch  ☑ Mobile home/chalet  ☐ Hotel/B&B  ☐ Apartment

In northern Portugal close to the Spanish border, this pleasant site is just 200 metres from the beach. It has an attractive and peaceful setting in woods alongside the river estuary that marks the border with Spain and on the edge of the little town of Caminha. The site is shaded by tall pines with other small trees planted to mark large sandy pitches. The main site road is surfaced but elsewhere take care not to get trapped in soft sand. Pitching and parking can be haphazard. Static units are grouped together on one side of the site. Water points, electrical supply and lighting are good. With a pleasant, open feel about the setting, fishing is possible in the estuary, and swimming, either there or from the rather open, sandy beach.

## You might like to know
Fishing is possible both at the river estuary and from the attractive Caminha beach.

- ☑ Coarse fishing
- ☐ Fly fishing
- ☐ Sea fishing
- ☐ Lake on site
- ☐ River on site
- ☐ Lake nearby (max 5 km)
- ☑ River nearby (max 5 km)
- ☑ Licence / permit required
- ☐ Equipment hire available
- ☐ Bait and fishing supplies

**Facilities:** The clean, well maintained toilet block has British style toilets, washbasins (cold water) and hot showers, plus beach showers, extra dishwashing and laundry sinks (cold water). Laundry. Motorcaravan services. Supermarket. Small restaurant/bar with snacks (all Easter and 1/6-15/9). Bicycle hire. Off site: Beach 200 m. Fishing 200 m. Bus service 800 m.

**Open:** All year.

**Directions:** From the north, turn off the main coast road (N13-E50) just after camping sign at end of embankment alongside estuary, about 1.5 km. south of ferry. From the south on the N13 turn left at Hotel Faz de Minho at start of estuary and follow for 1 km. through woods to site. GPS: 41.86635, -8.85844

### Charges guide

| | |
|---|---|
| Per person | € 2,50 - € 4,50 |
| child (5-10 yrs) | € 1,30 - € 2,50 |
| caravan and car | € 5,60 - € 10,20 |
| electricity | € 2,50 - € 3,10 |

Off season discounts (up to 70%).

# Orbitur Camping São Jacinto

EN327 km 20, São Jacinto, P-3800-909 Aveiro (Aveiro)
t: **234 838 284**  e: **info@orbitur.pt**
alanrogers.com/PO8050  www.orbitur.pt

Accommodation: ☑Pitch  ☑Mobile home/chalet  ☐Hotel/B&B  ☐Apartment

This small site is in the São Jacinto nature reserve, on a peninsula between the Atlantic and the Barrinha, with views to the mountains beyond. The area is a weekend resort for locals and can be crowded in high season – it may therefore be difficult to find space in July/Aug, particularly for larger units. This is not a large site, taking 169 units on unmarked pitches, but in most places trees provide natural limits and shade. Swimming and fishing are both possible in the adjacent Ria, or the sea, a 20 minute walk from a guarded back gate. There is a private jetty for boats and the manager will organise hire of the decorative 'Moliceiros' boats used in days gone by to harvest seaweed for the land. A deep borehole supplies the site with drinking water.

## You might like to know
An evening stroll along the São Jacinto dunes is highly recommended.

☑ **Coarse fishing**
☐ **Fly fishing**
☑ **Sea fishing**
☐ **Lake on site**
☐ **River on site**
☐ **Lake nearby (max 5 km)**
☑ **River nearby (max 5 km)**
☑ **Licence / permit required**
☐ **Equipment hire available**
☐ **Bait and fishing supplies**

**Facilities:** Two toilet blocks, very clean when inspected, contain the usual facilities. Dishwashing and laundry sinks. Washing machine and ironing board in a separate part of the toilet block. Motorcaravan services. Shop. Restaurant, bar and snack bar (Easter, June-Oct). Attractive new playground. Five bungalows to rent. Off site: Bus service 20 m. Fishing 200 m. Bicycle hire 10 km.

**Open:** 1 January - 6 October.

**Directions:** Turn off the N109 at Estarreja to N109-5 to cross bridge over Ria da Gosta Nova and on to Torreira and São Jacinto. From Porto go south N1/09, turn for Ovar on the N327 which leads to São Jacinto.
GPS: 40.67497, -8.72295

### Charges guide

| | |
|---|---|
| Per person | € 4,30 |
| child (5-10 yrs) | € 2,20 |
| pitch | € 11,40 |
| electricity | € 2,90 - € 3,50 |

Off season discounts (up to 70%).

# Orbitur Camping Mira

Estrada Florestal no 1 km 2, Dunas de Mira, P-3070-792 Praia de Mira (Coimbra)
t: **231 471 234**  e: info@orbitur.pt
alanrogers.com/PO8070  www.orbitur.pt

**Accommodation:** ☑Pitch ☑Mobile home/chalet ☐Hotel/B&B ☐Apartment

A small, peaceful seaside site set in pinewoods, Orbitur Camping Mira is situated to the south of Aveiro and Vagos, in a quieter and less crowded area. It fronts onto a lake at the head of the Ria de Mira, which eventually runs into the Aveiro Ria. A back gate leads directly to the sea and a wide quiet beach 300 m. away. A road runs alongside the site boundary where the restaurant complex is situated, resulting in some road noise. The site has around 225 pitches on sand, which are not marked, but with trees that create natural divisions. Electricity and water points are plentiful. The site provides an inexpensive restaurant, snack bar, lounge bar and TV lounge. A medium sized supermarket is well stocked, with plenty of fresh produce. The Mira Ria is fascinating, with the brightly painted, decorative 'moliceiros' (traditional fishing boats).

## You might like to know

The Lagoa-Barrinha is an ideal spot for windsurfing, sailing, water skiing and rowing. Don't miss the striped wooden houses at Costa Nova.

- ☑ Coarse fishing
- ☐ Fly fishing
- ☑ Sea fishing
- ☐ Lake on site
- ☐ River on site
- ☑ Lake nearby (max 5 km)
- ☐ River nearby (max 5 km)
- ☑ Licence / permit required
- ☐ Equipment hire available
- ☐ Bait and fishing supplies

**Facilities:** The modern toilet blocks are clean, with 14 free hot showers and washing machines. Facilities for disabled visitors. Motorcaravan services. Gas supplies. Shop. Restaurant, bar and snack bar (Easter, June-Oct). TV room. Play area. Bicycle hire. WiFi at the bar. Bungalows (7) to rent. Off site: Bus service 150 m. (summer only). Fishing 500 m. Indoor pool, lake swimming and riding at Mira 7 km.

**Open:** 1 January - 30 November.

**Directions:** Take the IP5 (A25) southwest to Aveiro then the A17 south to Figuera da Foz. Then take the N109 north to Mira and follow signs west to Praia (beach) de Mira.
GPS: 40.4533, -8.79902

**Charges guide**

| | |
|---|---|
| Per person | € 4,90 |
| child (5-10 yrs) | € 2,50 |
| pitch | € 8,60 - € 11,90 |
| electricity | € 2,90 - € 3,50 |

Off season discounts (up to 70%).

ITALY – Rasen

# Camping Corones

I-39030 Rasen (Trentino - Alto Adige)
t: 047 449 6490  e: info@corones.com
alanrogers.com/IT61990  www.corones.com

Accommodation: ☑Pitch ☑Mobile home/chalet ☐Hotel/B&B ☑Apartment

Situated in a pine forest clearing at the foot of the attractive Antholz valley in the heart of German-speaking Südtirol, Corones is ideally situated both for winter sports enthusiasts and for walkers, cyclists, mountain bikers and those who prefer to explore the valleys and mountain roads of the Dolomites by car. There are 135 level pitches, all with electricity (16A) and many also with water, drainage and satellite TV. The Residence offers luxury apartments and there are authentic Canadian log cabins for hire. The bar/restaurant and small shop are open all season. From the site you can see slopes which in winter become highly rated skiing pistes. A short drive up the broad Antholz (Anterselva) valley takes you to an internationally important biathlon centre. A not-so-young British couple who were on site when we visited had just driven up the valley and over the pass into Austria and then back via another pass. Back on site, a small pool and paddling pool could be very welcome. There is a regular programme of free excursions and occasional evening events are organised.

## Special offers
Special family deals. Children's activity programme in Summer.

## You might like to know
There is something for everyone here: tranquil spots for those wanting to relax in the fresh air, and many opportunities for those looking for activities and adventure.

☑ Coarse fishing
☐ Fly fishing
☐ Sea fishing
☐ Lake on site
☐ River on site
☑ Lake nearby (max 5 km)
☑ River nearby (max 5 km)
☑ Licence / permit required
☐ Equipment hire available
☐ Bait and fishing supplies

**Facilities:** The central toilet block is traditional but well maintained and clean. Additional facilities below the Residence are of the highest quality including individual shower rooms with washbasins, washbasins with all WCs, a delightful children's unit and an excellent facility for disabled visitors. Luxurious wellness centre with saunas, solarium, jacuzzis, massage, therapy pools and heat benches. Heated outdoor swimming and paddling pools (4/5-20/10). Play area. Internet facilities. Off site: Tennis 800 m. Bicycle hire 1 km. Riding and fishing 3 km. Golf (9 holes) 10 km. Canoeing/kayaking 15 km.

**Open:** 6 December - 30 March and 4 May - 31 October.

**Directions:** Rasen/Rasun is 85 km. northeast of Bolzano. From Bressanone/Brixen exit on the A22 Brenner - Modena motorway, go east on SS49 for 50 km. then turn north (signed Razen/Antholz). Turn immediately west at roundabout in Niederrasen/Rasun di Sotto to site on left in 100 m.  GPS: 46.7758, 12.0367

### Charges guide

| Per unit incl. 2 persons, electricity on meter | € 19,70 - € 28,80 |
|---|---|
| extra person | € 4,60 - € 7,80 |
| child (3-15 yrs) | € 3,00 - € 7,20 |

# Caravan Park Sexten

Saint Josef Strasse 54, I-39030 Sexten (Trentino - Alto Adige)
t: 047 471 0444   e: info@parksexten.com
alanrogers.com/IT62030   www.parksexten.com

Accommodation: ☑Pitch  ☑Mobile home/chalet  ☐Hotel/B&B  ☐Apartment

Caravan Park Sexten is 1,520 metres above sea level and has 268 pitches, some very large and all with electricity (16A) and TV connections, and with water and drainage in summer and winter (underground heating stops pipes freezing). Some pitches are in the open to catch the sun, others are tucked in forest clearings by the river. They are mostly gravelled to provide an ideal all-year surface. It is the facilities that make this a truly remarkable site; no expense or effort has been spared to create a luxurious environment that matches that of any top class hotel. The brand new health spa has every type of sauna, Turkish and Roman baths, sunbeds, herbal and hay baths, hairdressing and beauty treatment salons, relaxation and massage rooms and a remarkable indoor pool with children's pool, Kneipp therapy pool and whirlpools. The timber of the buildings is from 400 year old farmhouses and is blended with top quality modern materials to create amazing interiors and (mainly) authentic Tyrolean exteriors. The restaurant, bars and taverna are of equally high quality. Member of Leading Campings Group.

## You might like to know

Another great service here is the in-house car hire facility. Simply book at reception, pick up your keys and you are ready to go.

- ☑ Coarse fishing
- ☐ Fly fishing
- ☐ Sea fishing
- ☐ Lake on site
- ☑ River on site
- ☐ Lake nearby (max 5 km)
- ☐ River nearby (max 5 km)
- ☑ Licence / permit required
- ☐ Equipment hire available
- ☐ Bait and fishing supplies

**Facilities:** The three main toilet blocks are remarkable in design, fixtures and fittings. Heated floors. Controllable showers. Hairdryers. Luxurious private facilities to rent. Children and baby rooms. En-suite facilities for disabled visitors. Laundry and drying room. Motorcaravan services. Shop. Bars and restaurants with entertainment 2-3 nights a week. Indoor pool. Heated outdoor pool (1/6-30/9). High quality health spa. Good range of activities for all. Tennis. Bicycle hire. Climbing wall. Fishing. Adventure activity packages. Internet access and WiFi (whole site). Off site: Skiing in winter (free bus to 2 ski lifts within 5 km. Walking, cycling and climbing. Fishing. Riding and golf nearby.

**Open:** All year.

**Directions:** From Bressanone/Brixen exit on the A22 Brenner - Modena motorway follow the SS49 east for about 60 km. Turn south on the SS52 at Innichen/San Candido and follow signs to Sexten. Site is 5 km. past village (signed). GPS: 46.66727, 12.40221

### Charges guide

| | |
|---|---|
| Per person | € 7,00 - € 12,50 |
| child | € 1,00 - € 10,50 |
| pitch (80-280 m²) | € 5,00 - € 22,00 |
| electricity per kWh (16A) | € 0,70 |

# Camping Spiaggia Lago Caldonazzo

Viale Venezia, 12, I-38050 Calceranica al Lago (Trentino - Alto Adige)
t: **0461 723037**  e: **info@campingspiaggia.net**
alanrogers.com/IT62230  www.campingspiaggia.net

**Accommodation:** ☑Pitch  ☑Mobile home/chalet  ☐ Hotel/B&B  ☐ Apartment

Camping Spiaggia is a well organised site with a private, tree-lined beach on Lake Caldonazzo. The bar here, 'Miralago' can be found on the lakeshore, from where there is a beautiful panorama of the lake and surrounding mountains. This is a tranquil site, particularly in low season. In peak season, there is more activity with a twice weekly coach service taking teenagers to the nearest disco, 9 km. away. There are 104 pitches here, mostly well shaded and with electrical connections. A number of mobile homes are available for rent. Other on-site amenities include beach volleyball and a children's playground. Fishing and lake swimming are both understandably popular here, and a variety of water sports are on offer in the area, including windsurfing, sailing, canoeing and water skiing. Other more adventurous sports can also be organised such as rafting, canyoning or hydro speed. For adrenaline seekers, there is the 'Acropark', a tree top adventure park, close to Caldonazzo. Further afield, Venice, Verona and Padua are all possible day trips and the Calceranica Mine Museum is also worth a visit.

**Facilities:** Bar/restaurant and pizzeria. Direct lake access. Fishing. Windsurfing. Beach volleyball. Play area. Tourist information. Mobile homes for rent. Off site: Nearby resort of Caldonazzo (good selection of cafés, restaurants and shops). Walking and cycle routes. Adventure sports. Watersports.

**Open:** 16 April - 15 October.

**Directions:** Lake Caldonazzo lies to the east of the A22 autostrada. From Levico Terme, head west on SP1 to Caldonazzo and then follow signs to the site. GPS: 46.004343, 11.259763

**Charges guide**

| Per unit incl. 2 persons and electricity | € 18,50 - € 35,00 |
|---|---|
| extra person | € 5,50 - € 11,00 |
| child (3-12 yrs) | € 3,50 - € 7,00 |
| dog | € 3,00 |

## Special offers

April, May, June and September with this guide: € 15 per night for a touring pitch and two persons. € 40 per night for a mobile home (including 2 persons).

## You might like to know

Fishing licences can be bought at the reception. A little fishing boat is available for campsite guests.

☑ **Coarse fishing**
☐ **Fly fishing**
☐ **Sea fishing**
☑ **Lake on site**
☐ **River on site**
☐ **Lake nearby (max 5 km)**
☑ **River nearby (max 5 km)**
☑ **Licence / permit required**
☐ **Equipment hire available**
☐ **Bait and fishing supplies**

# Camping Lévico

Localitá Pleina 5, I-38056 Lévico Terme (Trentino - Alto Adige)
t: 046 170 6491  e: mail@campinglevico.com
alanrogers.com/IT62290  www.campinglevico.com

**Accommodation:** ☑Pitch ☑Mobile home/chalet ☐ Hotel/B&B ☐ Apartment

Sister site to Camping Jolly, Camping Lévico is in a natural setting on the small, very pretty Italian lake also called Lévico, which is surrounded by towering mountains. The sites are owned by two brothers – Andrea, who manages Lévico, and Gino, based at Jolly. Both campsites are charming. Lévico has some pitches along the lake edge and a quiet atmosphere. There is a shaded terrace for enjoying pizza and drinks in the evening. Pitches are of a good size, most grassed and well shaded with 6A electricity. Staff are welcoming and fluent in many languages, including English. There is a small supermarket on site and it is a short distance to the local village. The beautiful grass shores of the lake are ideal for sunbathing and the crystal clear water is ideal for enjoying (non-motorised) water activities. This is a site where the natural beauty of an Italian lake can be enjoyed without being overwhelmed by commercial tourism. All the amenities at Camping Jolly can be enjoyed by traversing a very pretty walkway along a stream where we saw many trout.

## You might like to know

Large private beach. As well as fishing, the clear, shallow waters of the lake offer opportunities for swimming, canoeing, and boating. You can rent canoes and pedal boats from reception.

☑ Coarse fishing
☐ Fly fishing
☐ Sea fishing
☑ Lake on site
☑ River on site
☑ Lake nearby (max 5km)
☑ River nearby (max 5km)
☑ Licence / permit required
☐ Equipment hire available
☐ Bait and fishing supplies

**Facilities:** Four modern sanitary blocks provide hot water for showers, washbasins and washing. Mostly British style toilets. Single locked unit for disabled visitors. Washing machines and dryer. Ironing. Freezer. Motorcaravan service point. Bar/restaurant, takeaway and good shop. Play area. Miniclub and entertainment (high season). Fishing. Satellite TV and cartoon cinema. Internet access. Kayak hire. Tennis. Torches useful. Off site: Town 2 km. with all the usual facilities and ATM. Bicycle hire 1.5 km. and bicycle track. Boat launching 500 m. Riding 3 km. Golf 7 km.

**Open:** 1 April - 11 October.

**Directions:** From A22 Verona - Bolzano road take turn for Trento on S47 to Lévico Terme where campsite is very well signed. GPS: 46.00799, 11.28454

### Charges guide

| | |
|---|---|
| Per person | € 5,00 - € 9,50 |
| child (3-11 yrs) | € 4,00 - € 6,00 |
| pitch incl. electricity (6A) | € 7,50 - € 18,00 |

ITALY – Pacengo

# Camping Lido

Via Peschiera 2, I-37017 Pacengo (Lake Garda)
t: 045 759 0611  e: info@campinglido.it
alanrogers.com/IT62540  www.campinglido.it

**Accommodation:** ☑ Pitch  ☑ Mobile home/chalet  ☐ Hotel/B&B  ☐ Apartment

Camping Lido is one of the largest and amongst the best of the 120 campsites around Lake Garda and is situated at the southeast corner of the lake. There is quite a slope from the entrance down to the lake so many of the 683 grass touring pitches are on terraces, which give lovely views across the lake. They are of varying sizes, separated by hedges, all have electrical connections and 57 are fully serviced. This is a most attractive site with tall, neatly trimmed trees standing like sentinels on either side of the broad avenue which runs from the entrance right down to the lake. A wide variety of trees provide shade on some pitches and flowers add colour to the overall appearance. Near the top of the site is a large, well designed pool with a paddling pool and slides into splash pools. The site has its own beach with a landing stage that marks off a large area for swimming on one side and on the other an area where boats can be moored. One could happily spend all the holiday here without leaving the site but with so many attractions nearby this would be a pity.

## You might like to know
Gardaland is Italy's premier theme park and is within easy reach of this site.

☑ Coarse fishing
☐ Fly fishing
☐ Sea fishing
☑ Lake on site
☐ River on site
☐ Lake nearby (max 5 km)
☑ River nearby (max 5 km)
☑ Licence / permit required
☐ Equipment hire available
☐ Bait and fishing supplies

**Facilities:** Seven modern toilet blocks (three heated) include provision for disabled visitors and three family rooms. Washing machines and dryer. Fridge rental. Restaurant, bars, pizzeria, takeaway and well stocked supermarket. Swimming pool, paddling pool and slides. Superb fitness centre. Playground. Tennis. Bicycle hire. Watersports. Fishing. Activity programme (high season). Shingle beach with landing stage and mooring for boats. Dogs are not accepted in high season (5/7-15/8). Off site: Bus 200 m. Gardaland theme park.

**Open:** 20 March - 11 October.

**Directions:** Leave A4 Milan - Venice motorway at exit for Peschiera. Head north on east side of lake on the SS249. Site entrance on left after Gardaland theme park.
GPS: 45.46996, 10.72042

### Charges guide

| | |
|---|---|
| Per person | € 4,50 - € 7,00 |
| child (3-5 yrs) | € 3,00 - € 4,10 |
| pitch incl. services | € 8,60 - € 17,00 |

# Camping Villaggio Italgest

Via Martiri di Cefalonia, I-06063 Sant Arcangelo-Magione (Umbria)
t: 075 848 238   e: camping@italgest.com
alanrogers.com/IT66520   www.italgest.com

Accommodation: ☑Pitch  ☑Mobile home/chalet  ☐ Hotel/B&B  ☐ Apartment

Directly on the shore on the south side of Lake Trasimeno, which is almost midway between the Mediterranean and the Adriatic, Sant Arcangelo is ideally placed for exploring Umbria and Tuscany. The area around the lake is fairly flat and has views of the distant hills, but can become very hot during summer. Villaggio Italgest is a pleasant site with 208 touring pitches on level grass and, except for the area next to the lake, under a cover of tall trees. All pitches have electrical connections and cars are parked away from the pitches. The site offers a wide variety of activities and tours are organised daily. There is entertainment for children and adults in high season, including Italian language and civilisation courses. The bar/disco remains open until 02.00. There is a good sized swimming pool area, one pool with slides, a smaller paddling pool and a whirlpool. The site has a marina for boats with a crane. Whether you wish to use this site as a base for exploration or as a place to relax, you will find this a most pleasant place to stay. English is spoken.

## You might like to know

This sites location makes it an excellent base for trips to famous art cities such as Rome, Florence, Siena, Perugia, Assisi and Orvieto.

- ☑ Coarse fishing
- ☐ Fly fishing
- ☐ Sea fishing
- ☑ Lake on site
- ☐ River on site
- ☐ Lake nearby (max 5 km)
- ☑ River nearby (max 5 km)
- ☑ Licence / permit required
- ☑ Equipment hire available
- ☐ Bait and fishing supplies

**Facilities:** The one large and two smaller sanitary blocks have mainly British style WCs and free hot water in the washbasins and showers. Facilities for disabled visitors. Motorcaravan services. Washing machines and dryers. Kitchen. Bar, restaurant, pizzeria and takeaway (all season). Shop. Recently enlarged swimming pool. Tennis. Play area. TV (satellite) and games rooms. Disco. Films. Watersports, motorboat hire and lake swimming. Fishing. Mountain bike and scooter hire. Internet point. Activities, entertainment and excursions. Off site: Golf, parachuting, riding, canoeing and sailing close.

**Open:** 1 April - 30 September.

**Directions:** Site is on the southern shore of Lake Trasimeno. Take Magione exit from the Perugia spur of the Florence - Rome autostrada, proceed southwest round the lake to S. Arcangelo where site is signed. GPS: 43.08633, 12.15383

## Charges guide

| Per unit incl. 2 persons and electricity | € 18,00 - € 28,50 |
|---|---|
| extra person | € 6,00 - € 8,50 |
| child (3-9 yrs) | € 4,00 - € 6,50 |
| dog | € 2,00 - € 2,50 |

# Kamp Koren Kobarid

Drenzniske Ravne 33, SLO-5222 Kobarid
t: 053 891 311  e: info@kamp-koren.si
alanrogers.com/SV4270  www.kamp-koren.si

**Accommodation:** ☑Pitch ☑Mobile home/chalet ☐Hotel/B&B ☐Apartment

The campsite, run to perfection by Lidija Koren, occupies a flat, tree-lined meadow on a wide ledge which drops down sharply to the Soca river and a new, terraced area behind reception. A small site with just 60 pitches, it is deservedly very popular with those interested in outdoor sports, including paragliding, canoeing, canyoning, rafting and fishing. Equally, a pleasant atmosphere is generated for those seeking a quiet and relaxing break. New in 2009, wooden bungalows (sleeping two and four). The Julian Alps, and in particular the Triglav National Park, is a wonderful and under-explored part of Slovenia that has much to offer. Kobarid, probably best approached via Udine in Italy, is a pleasant country town, with easy access to nearby rivers, valleys and mountains which alone justify a visit to Kamp Koren. But most British visitors will remember it for the opportunity it provides to fill that curious gap in their knowledge of European history. The excellent museum in Kobarid was voted European Museum of the year recently.

## Special offers
A wide programme of activities, with 20% discount on water sports and free sauna for anyone staying longer than seven nights. You can also purchase fishing permits on site.

## You might like to know
Located near the most interesting spots in the Soca valley: the river canyon, the Kozjak waterfall, gravel pits, Napoleon's bridge and the restored front-line from World War I.

☑ Coarse fishing
☐ Fly fishing
☐ Sea fishing
☐ Lake on site
☑ River on site
☐ Lake nearby (max 5km)
☐ River nearby (max 5km)
☑ Licence / permit required
☑ Equipment hire available
☑ Bait and fishing supplies

**Facilities:** Two attractive log-built toilet blocks are of a standard worthy of a high class private sports club. Facilities for disabled visitors. Laundry facilities. Motorcaravan services. Shop (March-Nov). Café dispenses light meals, snacks and drinks apparently without much regard to closing hours. Sauna. Play area. Bowling. Fishing. Bicycle hire. Canoe hire. Climbing walls for adults. Off site: Town within walking distance. Riding 5 km. Golf 20 km. Guided tours in the Soca valley and around Slovenia start from the site.

**Open:** All year.

**Directions:** Site is on a side road that leads east out of Kobarid towards Bovec, just beyond so-called Napoleon's Bridge, well signed on the left.  GPS: 46.25075, 13.58658

### Charges guide

| | |
|---|---|
| Per person | € 9,50 - € 11,00 |
| child (7-13 yrs) | € 4,75 - € 5,50 |
| electricity | € 4,00 |
| dog | € 2,00 |

# Camping Sobec

Sobceva cesta 25, SLO-4248 Lesce
t: 045 353 700  e: sobec@siol.net
alanrogers.com/SV4210

**Accommodation:** ☑Pitch ☑Mobile home/chalet ☐ Hotel/B&B ☐ Apartment

Sobec is situated in a valley between the Julian Alps and the Karavanke Mountains, in a pine grove between the Sava Dolinka river and a small lake. It is only 3 km. from Bled and 20 km. from the Karavanke Tunnel. There are 500 unmarked pitches on level, grassy fields off tarmac access roads (450 for touring units), all with 16A electricity. Shade is provided by mature pine trees and younger trees separate some pitches. Camping Sobec is surrounded by water – the Sava river borders it on three sides and on the fourth is a small, artificial lake with grassy fields for sunbathing. Some pitches have views over the lake, which has an enclosed area providing safe swimming for children. This site is a good base for an active holiday, since both the Sava Dolinka and the Sava Bohinjka rivers are suitable for canoeing, kayaking, rafting and fishing, whilst the nearby mountains offer challenges for mountain climbing, paragliding and canyoning.

## Special offers
Special 20% price reduction to fishing guests staying in Alan Rogers Award-winning bungalows or camping on regular pitches.

## You might like to know
Camping Sobec reception desk features a complete selection of fishing permits for all nearby rivers and lakes. There are a number of keen anglers amongst the site staff, who will be more than happy to give you a few local hints. www.fly-fishing-slovenia.si.

☐ Coarse fishing
☑ Fly fishing
☐ Sea fishing
☑ Lake on site
☑ River on site
☑ Lake nearby (max 5 km)
☑ River nearby (max 5 km)
☑ Licence / permit required
☑ Equipment hire available
☑ Bait and fishing supplies

**Facilities:** Three traditional style toilet blocks (all refurbished) with mainly British style toilets, washbasins in cabins and controllable hot showers. Child size toilets and basins. Well equipped baby room. Facilities for disabled visitors. Laundry facilities. Motorcaravan service point. Supermarket, bar/restaurant with stage for live performances. Playgrounds. Rafting, canyoning and kayaking organised. Miniclub. Tours to Bled and the Triglav National Park organised. Off site: Golf and riding 2 km.

**Open:** 21 April - 30 September.

**Directions:** Site is off the main road from Lesce to Bled and is well signed just outside Lesce. GPS: 46.35607, 14.14992

**Charges guide**

| Per unit incl. 2 persons and electricity | € 24,80 - € 29,00 |
| --- | --- |
| extra person | € 10,70 - € 12,80 |
| child (7-14 yrs) | € 8,00 - € 9,60 |
| dog | € 3,50 |

# Balatontourist Levendula Naturist

Hókuli u. 25., H-8243 Balatonakali (Veszprem)
t: **87 544 011**  e: **levendula@balatontourist.hu**
alanrogers.com/HU5385  www.balatontourist.hu

Accommodation: ☑Pitch ☑Mobile home/chalet ☐ Hotel/B&B ☐ Apartment

Levendula is a naturist site and is the latest addition to the Balatontourist chain of sites on the north side of Lake Balaton. It has 108 level, unmarked pitches, varying in size from 60-120 m², and separated by low hedges. Almost all have views of the lake and all have electricity (4/10A). The site is attractively landscaped with shrubs and flowers and there is direct access to the lake. As part of the Balatontourist organisation, Levendula has similar amenities to the other sites, including a full entertainment program for children in high season, but without the noise of its larger brothers. The new toilet buildings are worth mentioning – they are among the best we have seen in Central Europe. The north side of Lake Balaton has much to offer culturally. Veszprém county has a rich history with baroque towns, castles, old churches. Local items of interest include a watermill and the Protestant cemetery from the first decades of the 19th century with its heart shaped tombs.

## You might like to know

Lake Balaton is the biggest freshwater lake in Europe with a coastline of 200 km. The best-known fish from the lake is the zander, which is also known as Balaton zander.

☑ Coarse fishing
☐ Fly fishing
☐ Sea fishing
☑ Lake on site
☐ River on site
☐ Lake nearby (max 5 km)
☐ River nearby (max 5 km)
☑ Licence / permit required
☐ Equipment hire available
☐ Bait and fishing supplies

**Facilities:** Two toilet blocks with modern fittings, including one washbasin in a cabin for men and women. Facilities for disabled visitors. Heated baby room. Laundry. Campers' kitchen with cooking rings on request. Fish cleaning area. Dog shower. Bar/restaurant with terrace. Shop. Playground with colourful equipment. Watersports. Games room. Animation programme. Excursions. Off site: Riding 1.5 km.

**Open:** 12 May - 10 September.

**Directions:** Follow no. 71 road towards Keszthely and site is signed in Balatonakali. GPS: 46.87933, 17.74225

**Charges guide**

| Per unit incl. 2 persons and electricity | HUF 3500 - 6800 |
| --- | --- |
| extra person | HUF 850 - 1200 |
| child (2-14 yrs) | HUF 650 - 950 |
| dog | HUF 650 - 950 |

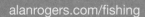

# Martfü Health & Recreation Centre

Tüzép utca, H-5435 Martfü (Jász-Nagkyun-Szolnok County)
t: **56 580531**  e: **martfu@camping.hu**
alanrogers.com/HU5255  www.martfu-turizmus.hu

**Accommodation:** ☑Pitch ☑Mobile home/chalet ☐Hotel/B&B ☐Apartment

The Martfü campsite is new and modern with 61 tourist pitches on newly developed, grassy terrain with rubber hardstandings. Each of around 90 m² and separated by young bushes and trees, all have electricity (16/25A), waste water drainage, cable and satellite TV. There is a water tap per two pitches. There is no shade as yet, which may cause the site to become a real suntrap in summer, when temperatures may rise up to 34 degrees. A small lake and its beach on the site will cool you off. The main attraction at this site is the thermal spa (still under construction when we visited) which is said to aid people with dermal and rheumatic problems. Martfü is right on the banks of the River Tisza, which also makes it an excellent spot for those who enjoy watersports and fishing. The village of Martfü is close with numerous shops, restaurants and bars.

## You might like to know

The Tisza is Europe's 16th longest river, rising in the Ukraine and winding through much of central Europe before joining the Danube in Serbia.

☑ Coarse fishing
☐ Fly fishing
☐ Sea fishing
☐ Lake on site
☑ River on site
☐ Lake nearby (max 5 km)
☐ River nearby (max 5 km)
☑ Licence / permit required
☐ Equipment hire available
☐ Bait and fishing supplies

**Facilities:** Two modern, heated toilet blocks with British style toilets, open style washbasins, and free, controllable hot showers. Children's toilet and shower. Heated baby room. En-suite facilities for disabled visitors. Laundry. Kitchen with cooking rings. Motorcaravan services. Shop for basics. Takeaway for bread and drinks. Welcoming bar with satellite TV and internet. Bowling. Library. Sauna. Jacuzzi. Playing field. Tennis. Minigolf. Fishing. Bicycle hire. Watersports. English is spoken. Off site: Fishing 50 m. Riding 5 km. Boat launching 1,5 km.

**Open:** All year.

**Directions:** Driving into Martfü from the north on the 442 road, take the first exit at the roundabout (site is signed). Continue for about 800 m. and site is signed on the right.
GPS: 47.019933, 20.268517

### Charges guide

| | |
|---|---|
| Per person | HUF 1200 |
| child (5-14 yrs) | HUF 600 |
| pitch | HUF 900 - 1200 |
| electricity | HUF 250 |

No credit cards.

# Balatontourist Camping Napfény

Halász u. 5, H-8253 Révfülöp (Veszprem County)
t: 87 563 031   e: napfeny@balatontourist.hu
alanrogers.com/HU5370   www.balatontourist.hu

Accommodation: ☑Pitch  ☑Mobile home/chalet  ☐Hotel/B&B  ☐Apartment

Camping Napfény, an exceptionally good site, is designed for families with children of all ages looking for an active holiday, and has a 200 m. frontage on Lake Balaton. The site's 395 pitches vary in size (60-110 m²) and almost all have shade – very welcome during the hot Hungarian summers – and 6-10A electricity. As with most of the sites on Lake Balaton, a train line runs just outside the site boundary. There are steps to get into the lake and canoes, boats and pedaloes for hire. An extensive entertainment programme is designed for all ages and there are several bars and restaurants of various styles. There are souvenir shops and a supermarket. In fact, you need not leave the site at all during your holiday, although there are several excursions on offer, including to Budapest or to one of the many Hungarian spas, a trip over Lake Balaton or a wine tour.

## You might like to know
The campsite is within easy reach of Kali-basin, often considered to be the most beautiful countryside to the north of Lake Balaton.

☑ Coarse fishing
☐ Fly fishing
☐ Sea fishing
☑ Lake on site
☐ River on site
☐ Lake nearby (max 5 km)
☑ River nearby (max 5 km)
☑ Licence / permit required
☐ Equipment hire available
☐ Bait and fishing supplies

**Facilities:** The three excellent sanitary blocks have toilets, washbasins (open style and in cabins) with hot and cold water, spacious showers (both preset and controllable), child size toilets and basins, and two bathrooms (hourly charge). Heated baby room. Facilities for disabled visitors. Launderette. Dog shower. Motorcaravan services. Supermarket. Several bars, restaurants and souvenir shops. Sports field. Tennis. Minigolf. Fishing. Bicycle hire. Canoe, rowing boat and pedalo hire. Extensive entertainment programme for all ages. Free internet access. Off site: Riding 3 km.

**Open:** 30 April - 30 September.

**Directions:** Follow road 71 from Veszprém southeast to Keszthely. Site is in Révfülöp. GPS: 46.82417, 17.63733

**Charges guide**

| Per unit incl. 2 persons and electricity | HUF 3400 - 7150 |
|---|---|
| extra person | HUF 800 - 1200 |
| child (2-14 yrs) | HUF 550 - 900 |
| dog | HUF 550 - 900 |

# Sportcamp Woferlgut

Kroessenbach 40, A-5671 Bruck (Salzburg)
t: 065 457 3030  e: info@sportcamp.at
alanrogers.com/AU0180  www.sportcamp.at

**Accommodation:** ☑Pitch  ☑Mobile home/chalet  ☐ Hotel/B&B  ☐ Apartment

The village of Bruck lies at the junction of the B311 and the Grossglocknerstrasse in the Hohe Tauern National Park. Sportcamp Woferlgut, a family run site, is one of the best in Austria. Surrounded by mountains, the site is quite flat with pleasant views. The 350 level, grass pitches are marked out by shrubs (300 for touring units) and each has electricity (16A), water, drainage, cable TV socket and gas point. A high grass bank separates the site and the road. The site's own lake, used for swimming and fishing, is surrounded by a landscaped sunbathing area. The fitness centre has a fully equipped gym, whilst another building contains a sauna and cold dip, Turkish bath, solarium (all free) massage on payment and a bar. In summer there is a free activity programme, evenings with live music, club for children, weekly barbecues and guided cycle and mountain tours. In winter, a cross country skiing trail and toboggan run lead from the site and a free bus service is provided to nearby skiing facilities. Good English is spoken.

## You might like to know
The lake here covers 15,000 m² and is one of the main attractions. Many other fishing opportunities on local rivers.

☑ Coarse fishing
☐ Fly fishing
☐ Sea fishing
☑ Lake on site
☐ River on site
☐ Lake nearby (max 5 km)
☑ River nearby (max 5 km)
☑ Licence / permit required
☐ Equipment hire available
☐ Bait and fishing supplies

**Facilities:** Three modern sanitary blocks (the newest in a class of its own) have excellent facilities, including private cabins, underfloor heating and music. Washing machines and dryers. Facilities for disabled visitors. Family bathrooms for hire. Motorcaravan services. Well stocked shop. Bar, restaurant and takeaway. Small, heated outdoor pool and children's pool (01/05-30/9). Fitness centre. Two playgrounds, indoor play room and children's cinema. Tennis. Bicycle hire. Fishing. Watersports and lake swimming. Collection of small animals with pony rides for young children. WiFi. Off site: Skiing 2.5 km. Golf 3 km. Boat launching and sailing 3.5 km. Hiking and skiing (all year) nearby.

**Open:** All year.

**Directions:** Site is southwest of Bruck. From road B311, Bruck by-pass, take southern exit (Grossglockner) and site is signed from the junction of B311 and B107 roads (small signs). GPS: 47.2838, 12.81694

**Charges guide**

| Per unit incl. 2 persons and electricity (plus meter) | € 21,90 - € 34,50 |
|---|---|
| extra person | € 5,10 - € 8,20 |
| child (2-10 yrs) | € 4,10 - € 6,10 |
| dog | € 3,10 - € 4,30 |

# Park Grubhof

Nr. 39, A-5092 Saint Martin bei Lofer (Salzburg)
t: 065 888 237  e: home@grubhof.com
alanrogers.com/AU0265  www.grubhof.com

**Accommodation:** ☑Pitch ☑Mobile home/chalet ☐ Hotel/B&B ☐ Apartment

Park Grubhof is a well organised, spacious site in a very scenic riverside location. The 200 pitches, all with electricity (12A), have been carefully divided into separate areas for different types of visitor – dog owners, young people, families and groups, and a quiet area. There are now 150 very large pitches, all with electricity, water and drainage, along the bank of the Saalach river. Although new, the central building housing reception, a cosy inn, a shop with caféteria, as well as a super sauna and wellness area and some of the site's sanitary facilities, has been built in traditional Tyrolian style using in part materials hundreds of years old, reclaimed from old farmhouses. The result is most attractive. Some areas are wooded with plenty of shade, others are more open and there are some very attractive log cabins which have been rescued from the old logging camps. Many of the possible activities are based around the river, where you will find barbecue areas, canoeing and white water rafting, fishing and swimming (when the river level reduces). In winter, the ski resort of Lofer Alm is only 2 km. (free ski shuttle).

## You might like to know
Grubhof extends along the banks of the Saalach. A great place to enjoy the sounds of birdsong or the babble and rush of the river.

☑ Coarse fishing
☐ Fly fishing
☐ Sea fishing
☐ Lake on site
☑ River on site
☐ Lake nearby (max 5 km)
☐ River nearby (max 5 km)
☑ Licence / permit required
☐ Equipment hire available
☐ Bait and fishing supplies

**Facilities:** Two attractive, modern sanitary units built with plenty of glass and wood, give a good provision of all facilities. Large showers. Some washbasins in cubicles. Saunas, steam bath, massage, fitness room. Separate facilities for canoeists. Motorcaravan service point. Shop, restaurant and bar. WiFi. Playground. Games room. Children's playroom. Watersports. Cabins to rent. Off site: Lofer 1 km. Gorges and caves 5-7 km. Salzburg 40 minutes drive. Many marked walking and cycling trails. Mountain climbing. Skiing at Lofer Alm 2 km. (free ski shuttle), cross-country track 300 m. Swimming pools at Lofer (open all day in summer).

**Open:** All year.

**Directions:** From A12 exit 17 (south of Kufstein) take B178 east to St Johann in Tyrol, then continue on the B178 northwest to Lofer, then south on B311 towards Zell am See. Site is 200 m. after the Lagerhaus filling station on the left. GPS: 47.57498, 12.70497

## Charges guide

| Per unit incl. 2 persons and electricity | € 20,00 - € 29,00 |
|---|---|
| extra person | € 5,70 - € 7,20 |
| child (under 14 yrs) | € 3,70 - € 4,50 |

No credit cards.

AUSTRIA – Döbriach

# Komfort-Campingpark Burgstaller

Seefeldstrasse 16, A-9873 Döbriach (Carinthia)
t: 042 467 774   e: info@burgstaller.co.at
alanrogers.com/AU0480   www.komfortcamping.at

**Accommodation:** ☑Pitch ☑Mobile home/chalet ☐ Hotel/B&B ☐ Apartment

This is one of Austria's top sites in a beautiful location and with all the amenities you could want. You can always tell a true family run site by the attention to detail and this site oozes perfection. This is an excellent family site with a very friendly atmosphere, particularly in the restaurant in the evenings. Good English is spoken. The 600 pitches (560 for tourists) are on flat, well drained grass, backing onto hedges on either side of access roads. All fully serviced (including WiFi), they vary in size (45-120 m². ) and there are special pitches for motorcaravans. One pitch actually rotates and follows the sun during the course of the day! The latest sanitary block warrants an architectural award; all toilets have a TV and a pirate ship on the first floor of the children's area sounds its guns every hour. The site entrance is directly opposite the park leading to the bathing lido, to which campers have free access. There is also a heated swimming pool. Much activity is organised here, including games and competitions for children and special Easter and autumn events.

## You might like to know

A special discount card is available for all campers and includes such benefits as free access to the region's lakes, swimming pools and museums.

☑ Coarse fishing
☐ Fly fishing
☐ Sea fishing
☑ Lake on site
☐ River on site
☑ Lake nearby (max 5 km)
☑ River nearby (max 5 km)
☑ Licence / permit required
☐ Equipment hire available
☐ Bait and fishing supplies

**Facilities:** Three exceptionally good quality toilet blocks include washbasins in cabins, facilities for children and disabled visitors, dishwashers and underfloor heating for cool weather. Seven private rooms for rent (3 with jacuzzi baths). Motorcaravan services. Good restaurant with terrace (May-Oct). Shop (May-Sept). Bowling alley. Disco (July/Aug). TV room. Sauna and solarium. Two play areas (one for under 6s, the other for 6-12 yrs). Bathing and boating on lake. Special entrance rate for lake attractions. Fishing. Bicycle hire. Mountain bike area. Riding. Entertainment programmes. Covered stage and outdoor arena. Off site: Mountain walks, climbing and farm visits.

**Open:** 4 April - 5 November.

**Directions:** Leave A10 at exit 139 (Spittal, Millstätter) then proceed alongside northern shore of lake through Millstätter towards Döbriach. Just before Döbriach turn right and after 1 km. site is on left. GPS: 46.77151, 13.64918

### Charges guide

| Per unit incl. 2 persons and electricity | € 20,40 - € 32,50 |
| --- | --- |
| extra person | € 7,00 - € 10,00 |
| child (4-14 yrs) | € 5,00 - € 7,50 |
| dog | € 2,50 - € 3,00 |

# Camping Manor Farm 1

CH-3800 Interlaken-Thunersee (Bern)
t: **033 822 2264**  e: **manorfarm@swisscamps.ch**
alanrogers.com/CH9420  www.manorfarm.ch

**Accommodation:** ☑Pitch  ☑Mobile home/chalet  ☐ Hotel/B&B  ☐ Apartment

Manor Farm has been popular with British visitors for many years as this is one of the traditional touring areas of Switzerland. The flat terrain is divided entirely into 525 individual, numbered pitches which vary considerably both in size (60-100 m²) and price, with 4/13A electricity available and shade in some places. There are 144 equipped with electricity, water, drainage and 55 also have cable TV connections. Reservations are made although you should find space except perhaps in late July/early August, but the best places may then be taken. Around 50% of the pitches are taken by permanent or letting units and a tour operator's presence. The site lies outside the town on the northern side of the Thuner See, with most of the site between road and lake but with one part on the far side of the road. Interlaken is very much a tourist town but the area is rich in scenery, with innumerable mountain excursions and walks available. The lakes and Jungfrau railway are near at hand. Manor Farm is a large campsite, efficiently run with a minimum of formality and would suit those looking for an active family holiday.

## You might like to know

Fishing in Lake Thun is important enough to keep a handful of professional fishers employed. In 2001 the total catch was 53,000 kg.

- ☑ Coarse fishing
- ☐ Fly fishing
- ☐ Sea fishing
- ☑ Lake on site
- ☐ River on site
- ☑ Lake nearby (max 5 km)
- ☑ River nearby (max 5 km)
- ☑ Licence / permit required
- ☑ Equipment hire available
- ☑ Bait and fishing supplies

**Facilities:** Eight separate toilet blocks are practical, heated and fully equipped. They include free hot water for baths and showers. Twenty private toilet units are for rent. Laundry facilities. Motorcaravan services. Gas supplies. Excellent shop (1/4-15/10). Site-owned restaurant adjoining (1/3-30/11). Snack bar (July/Aug). TV room. Playground and paddling pool. Minigolf. Bicycle hire. Sailing and windsurfing school. Lake swimming. Boat hire (slipway for your own). Fishing. Entertainment programme in high season. Excursions. Max. 1 dog. WiFi (charged). Off site: Golf 500 m. (handicap card). Riding 3 km. Free bus to heated indoor and outdoor pools (free entry).

**Open:** All year.

**Directions:** Site is 3 km. west of Interlaken along the road running north of the Thuner See towards Thun. Follow signs for 'Camp 1'. From A8 (bypassing Interlaken) take exit 24 marked 'Gunten, Beatenberg', which is a spur road bringing close to site. GPS: 46.68509, 7.81222

**Charges guide**

| Per unit incl. 2 persons and electricity | CHF 37,00 - 63,50 |
|---|---|
| extra person | CHF 10,50 |
| child (6-15 yrs) | CHF 5,00 |

# Camping Aaregg

Seestrasse 28a, CH-3855 Brienz am See (Bern)
t: 033 951 1843  e: mail@aaregg.ch
alanrogers.com/CH9510  www.aaregg.ch

**Accommodation:** ☑Pitch ☑Mobile home/chalet ☐ Hotel/B&B ☐ Apartment

Brienz, in the Bernese Oberland, is a delightful little town on the lake of the same name and the centre of the Swiss wood carving industry. Camping Aaregg is an excellent site situated on the southern shores of the lake with splendid views across the water to the mountains. There are 65 static caravans occupying their own area and 180 touring pitches, all with electricity (10/16A). Of these, 16 are larger with hardstandings, water and drainage, and many have good lake views. Pitches that front the lake have a surcharge. The trees and flowers make an attractive and peaceful environment. An excellent base from which to explore the many attractions of this scenic region, and is a useful night stop when passing from Interlaken to Luzern. Nearby at Ballenberg is the fascinating Freilichtmuseum, a very large open-air park of old Swiss houses which have been brought from all over Switzerland and re-erected in groups. Traditional Swiss crafts are demonstrated in some of these.

## You might like to know
The Swiss capital, Bern, is within easy access. The old part of the city has featured on UNESCOs world heritage list since 1983.

- ☑ Coarse fishing
- ☐ Fly fishing
- ☐ Sea fishing
- ☑ Lake on site
- ☐ River on site
- ☐ Lake nearby (max 5 km)
- ☐ River nearby (max 5 km)
- ☑ Licence / permit required
- ☐ Equipment hire available
- ☐ Bait and fishing supplies

**Facilities:** New very attractive sanitary facilities built and maintained to first class standards. Showers with washbasins. Washbasins (open style and in cubicles). Children's section. Family shower rooms. Baby changing room. Facilities for disabled visitors. Laundry facilities. Motorcaravan services. Pleasant restaurant with terrace and takeaway in season. Play area. Fishing. Bicycle hire. Boat launching. Lake swimming in clear water (unsupervised). English is spoken. Off site: Frequent train services to Interlaken and Lucerne as well as boat cruises from Brienz to Interlaken and back. Motorboat hire is possible, and waterskiing on the lake.

**Open:** 1 April - 31 October.

**Directions:** Site is on road B6/B11 on the east of Brienz. Entrance is just about opposite the Esso filling station, well signed. From the Interlaken-Luzern motorway, take Brienz exit and turn towards Brienz, site then on the left. GPS: 46.75000, 8.03332

### Charges guide

| | |
|---|---|
| Per unit incl. 2 persons and electricity | CHF 34,40 - 59,00 |
| per person | CHF 7,70 - 11,00 |
| child (6-16 yrs) | CHF 4,90 - 7,00 |
| dog | CHF 2,80 - 4,00 |

# Camping Campofelice

Via alle Brere 7, CH-6598 Tenero (Ticino)
t: 091 745 1417  e: camping@campofelice.ch
alanrogers.com/CH9890  www.campofelice.ch

Accommodation: ☑Pitch ☑Mobile home/chalet ☐Hotel/B&B ☐Apartment

The largest site in Switzerland, it is bordered on the front by Lake Maggiore and on one side by the Verzasca estuary, where the site has its own harbour. Campofelice is divided into rows, with 860 individual pitches of average size on flat grass on either side of hard access roads. Mostly well shaded, all pitches have electricity connections (10-13A) and some also have water, drainage and TV connections. Pitches near the lake cost more (these are not available for motorcaravans) and a special area is reserved for small tents. Some pitches have minimum stay regulations applied. English is spoken at this good, if rather expensive, site. Sporting facilities are good and there are cycle paths in the area, including into Locarno. The beach by the lake is sandy, long and wider than the usual lakeside ones. It shelves gently so that bathing is safe for children.

## You might like to know
This excellent site is the largest in Switzerland.

- ☑ Coarse fishing
- ☐ Fly fishing
- ☐ Sea fishing
- ☑ Lake on site
- ☐ River on site
- ☐ Lake nearby (max 5 km)
- ☑ River nearby (max 5 km)
- ☑ Licence / permit required
- ☐ Equipment hire available
- ☐ Bait and fishing supplies

**Facilities:** The six toilet blocks (one heated) are of excellent quality. Washing machines and dryers. Motorcaravan services. Gas supplies. Supermarket, restaurant, bar and takeaway (all season). Tennis. Minigolf. Bicycle hire. Playground. Doctor calls. Dogs are not accepted Off site: Fishing 500 m. Water skiing and windsurfing 1 km. Riding 5 km. Golf 8 km.

**Open:** 18 March - 31 October.

**Directions:** On the Bellinzona - Locarno road 13, exit Tenero. Site is signed at roundabout. GPS: 46.168611, 8.855556

### Charges guide

| | |
|---|---|
| Per unit incl. 2 persons and electricity | CHF 38,00 - 82,00 |
| extra person | CHF 8,00 - 11,00 |

# Kawan Village les Mimosas

Chaussée de Mandirac, F-11100 Narbonne (Aude)
t: 04 68 49 03 72  e: info@lesmimosas.com
alanrogers.com/FR11070  www.lesmimosas.com

**Accommodation:** ☑Pitch  ☑Mobile home/chalet  ☐ Hotel/B&B  ☐ Apartment

Six kilometres inland from the beaches of Narbonne and Gruissan, this site benefits from a less hectic situation than others by the sea. The site is lively with plenty to amuse and entertain the younger generation whilst offering facilities for the whole family. A free club card is available in July/August to use the children's club, gym, sauna, tennis, minigolf, billiards etc. There are 250 pitches, 150 for touring, many in a circular layout of very good size, most with electricity (6A). There are a few 'grand confort', with reasonable shade, mostly from 2 m. high hedges. There is also a number of mobile homes and chalets to rent. This could be a very useful site offering many possibilities to meet a variety of needs, with on-site entertainment (including an evening on Cathar history), and easy access to popular beaches. Nearby Gruissan is a fascinating village with its wooden houses on stilts, beaches, ruined castle, port and salt beds. Narbonne has Roman remains and inland Cathar castles are to be found perched on rugged hill tops.

## You might like to know

Possible to fish on site without the need for a permit.

☑ Coarse fishing
☑ Fly fishing
☐ Sea fishing
☑ Lake on site
☐ River on site
☐ Lake nearby (max 5 km)
☐ River nearby (max 5 km)
☐ Licence / permit required
☐ Equipment hire available
☐ Bait and fishing supplies

**Facilities:** Sanitary buildings refurbished to a high standard. Washing machines. Shop and 'Auberge' restaurant (open all season). Takeaway. Bar. Small lounge, amusements (July/Aug). Landscaped heated pool with slides and islands (open 1/5), plus the original pool and children's pool (high season). New play area. Minigolf. Mountain bike hire. Tennis. Sauna, gym. Children's activities, sports, entertainment (high season). Bicycle hire. Multisports ground. Off site: Riding. Windsurfing/sailing school 300 m. Gruissan's beach 10 minutes. Lagoon, boating and fishing via footpath (200 m).

**Open:** 27 March - 1 November.

**Directions:** From A9 exit 38 (Narbonne Sud) take last exit on roundabout, back over the autoroute (site signed from here). Follow signs La Nautique and then Mandirac and site (6 km. from autoroute). Also signed from Narbonne centre. GPS: 43.13662, 3.02562

### Charges guide

| | |
|---|---|
| Per unit incl. 2 persons and electricity | € 17,50 - € 33,00 |
| incl. water and waste water | € 21,70 - € 38,00 |
| extra person | € 4,10 - € 10,00 |

FRANCE – Salles-Curan

# Kawan Village les Genêts

Lac de Pareloup, F-12410 Salles-Curan (Aveyron)
t: 05 65 46 35 34   e: contact@camping-les-genets.fr
alanrogers.com/FR12080   www.camping-les-genets.fr

Accommodation: ☑Pitch  ☑Mobile home/chalet  ☐ Hotel/B&B  ☐ Apartment

The 163 pitches include 80 grassy, mostly individual pitches for touring units. These are in two areas, one on each side of the entrance lane, and are divided by hedges, shrubs and trees. Most have electricity (6A) and many also have water and a waste water drain. The site slopes gently down to the beach and lake with facilities for all watersports including water skiing. A full animation and activities programme is organised in high season, and there is much to see and do in this very attractive corner of Aveyron. This family run site is on the shores of Lac de Pareloup and offers both family holidays and watersports facilities. The site is not suitable for American style motorhomes.

## You might like to know
Fishing lessons for children once a week.

☑ Coarse fishing
☐ Fly fishing
☐ Sea fishing
☑ Lake on site
☐ River on site
☐ Lake nearby (max 5 km)
☐ River nearby (max 5 km)
☑ Licence / permit required
☐ Equipment hire available
☑ Bait and fishing supplies

**Facilities:** Two sanitary units with suite for disabled visitors. The older unit has been refurbished. Baby room. Laundry. Well stocked shop. Bar, restaurant, snacks (main season). Swimming pool, spa pool (from 1/6; unsupervised). Playground. Minigolf. Boules. Bicycle hire. Pedaloes, windsurfers, kayaks. Fishing licences available. WiFi in bar.

**Open:** 31 May - 11 September.

**Directions:** From Salles-Curan take D577 for about 4 km. and turn right into a narrow lane immediately after a sharp right hand bend. Site is signed at junction.  GPS: 44.18933, 2.76693

### Charges guide

| | |
|---|---|
| Per unit incl. 2 persons and electricity | € 18,00 - € 39,00 |
| extra person | € 4,00 - € 7,50 |
| child (2-7 yrs) | free - € 7,00 |
| pet | € 3,00 - € 4,00 |

Refundable deposits for barrier card € 20 and for pool bracelet € 8 per person.

# Flower Camping Lac de Bonnefon

L'Etang de Bonnefon, F-12800 Naucelle (Aveyron)
t: 05 65 69 33 20  e: email-camping-du-lac-de-bonnefon@wanadoo.fr
alanrogers.com/FR12250  www.camping-du-lac-de-bonnefon.com

Accommodation: ☑Pitch ☑Mobile home/chalet ☐ Hotel/B&B ☐ Apartment

This small, family run site, popular with French campers, lies in a picturesque region waiting to be discovered, with rolling hills, deep river valleys, lakes and many old fortified villages. This site is more suitable for those seeking a quieter holiday with less in the way of entertainment. There are 112 good sized, grassy, slightly sloping pitches with 74 for touring (50 with 10A electricity). Some are separated by laurel hedging with others more open and maturing trees give a little shade. The new enthusiastic and friendly owners have recently extended the site and refurbished the facilities to a high standard. These improvements include new swimming and paddling pools with a large sunbathing terrace. This is a great area for touring by car, bike or on foot with many marked routes.

## You might like to know

Free fishing in the lake on site (no permit or licence required). Night fishing is not allowed.

- ☑ Coarse fishing
- ☐ Fly fishing
- ☐ Sea fishing
- ☑ Lake on site
- ☐ River on site
- ☐ Lake nearby (max 5 km)
- ☐ River nearby (max 5 km)
- ☐ Licence / permit required
- ☐ Equipment hire available
- ☑ Bait and fishing supplies

**Facilities:** Two toilet blocks include some washbasins in cabins and good facilities for disabled visitors. No shop but bread to order. Bar with TV (all season). Snack bar (July/Aug, other times on demand). Swimming and paddling pools (1/6-30/9). Playground. Archery. Good lake fishing but no bathing. Activities for all the family in July/Aug. Off site: Riding 500 m. Small village of Naucelle with a few shops and large heated pool complex 1 km.

**Open:** 1 April - 15 October.

**Directions:** Site is just off the N88 about halfway between Rodez and Albi. From Naucelle Gare take D997 towards Naucelle. In just over 1 km. turn left on D58 and follow signs to site in just under 1 km.  GPS: 44.18805, 2.34827

### Charges guide

| Per unit incl. 2 persons and electricity | € 15,50 - € 23,90 |
| --- | --- |
| extra person | € 3,50 - € 5,00 |
| child (2-10 yrs) | € 2,00 - € 3,00 |
| dog | € 2,50 |

# Kawan Village Chateau le Verdoyer

Champs Romain, F-24470 Saint Pardoux (Dordogne)
t: 05 53 56 94 64   e: chateau@verdoyer.fr
alanrogers.com/FR24010   www.verdoyer.fr

Accommodation: ☑Pitch   ☑Mobile home/chalet   ☐ Hotel/B&B   ☐ Apartment

The twenty six-hectare estate has three lakes, two for fishing and one with a sandy beach and safe swimming area. There are 135 good sized touring pitches, level, terraced and hedged. With a choice of wooded area or open field, all have electricity (5/10A) and most share a water supply between four pitches. There is a swimming pool complex and in high season activities are organised for children (5-13 yrs) but there is no disco. This site is well adapted for those with disabilities, with two fully adapted chalets, wheelchair access to all facilities and even a lift into the pool. Le Verdoyer has been developed in the park of a restored château and is owned by a Dutch family. We particularly like this site for its beautiful buildings and lovely surroundings. It is situated in the lesser known area of the Dordogne, sometimes referred to as the Périgord Vert, with its green forests and small lakes. The courtyard area between reception and the bar houses evening activities, and is a pleasant place to enjoy drinks and relax. The château itself has rooms to let and its excellent lakeside restaurant is also open to the public.

## You might like to know

Plenty to do on site – football, tennis, pétanque, ping pong, volleyball, basketball and mountain biking. Nearby, you can go canoeing, horse riding, play golf, ramble, karting, paint ball, vélo rail and much more.

- ☑ Coarse fishing
- ☐ Fly fishing
- ☐ Sea fishing
- ☑ Lake on site
- ☐ River on site
- ☐ Lake nearby (max 5 km)
- ☐ River nearby (max 5 km)
- ☐ Licence / permit required
- ☑ Equipment hire available
- ☑ Bait and fishing supplies

**Facilities:** Well appointed toilet blocks include facilities for disabled visitors, and baby baths. Serviced launderette. Motorcaravan services. Fridge rental. Shop with gas (1/5-30/9). Bar, snacks, takeaway and restaurant (1/5-30/9). Bistro (July/Aug). Two pools the smaller covered in low season, slide, paddling pool. Play areas. Tennis. Minigolf. Bicycle hire. Small library. WiFi (charged), Computer in reception for internet access. International newspapers daily. Off site: Riding 5 km. 'Circuit des Orchidées' (22 species of orchid). Market (Thur and Sun) at Saint Pardoux 12 km.

**Open:** 23 April - 6 October.

**Directions:** Site is 2 km. from the Limoges (N21) - Chalus (D6bis-D85) - Nontron road, 20 km. south of Chalus and is well signed from the main road. Site is on the D96 about 4 km. north of village of Champs Romain. GPS: 45.55035, 0.7947

**Charges guide**

| Per unit incl. 2 persons and electricity | € 21,00 - € 32,00 |
| --- | --- |
| extra person | € 5,00 - € 6,50 |
| child (6-11 yrs) | € 4,00 - € 5,00 |
| dog | free - € 4,00 |

# Camping du Lac de Groléjac

Le Roc Percé, F-24250 Groléjac (Dordogne)
t: 05 53 59 48 70  e: contact@camping-dulac-dordogne.com
alanrogers.com/FR24850  www.camping-dulac-dordogne.com

**Accommodation:** ☑Pitch ☑Mobile home/chalet ☐Hotel/B&B ☐Apartment

Mme. and M. Aubry purchased this former municipal site just over a year ago and an improvement plan covering the next few years is already underway. There are 92 pitches, 78 for touring, with electricity on 70 of them. There are also mobile homes and tent bungalows for rent. The pitches are delightfully positioned in a circular formation, the toilet and shower block being at the hub. Shady or sunny they are of a good size and divided by trees, shrubs and bamboo. By the side of a large lake, which is directly accessible from the site, swimming from the sandy beach area is supervised in high season by a lifeguard. The aim of the new owners is to provide a haven of peace where you can enjoy the luxuriant nature surrounding the lake and from where you can discover this wonderful region. In July and August the facilities at the lake are free of charge to campers and much of the equipment needed is available at reception. A swimming pool and a permanent building for a snack bar and bar with decking are planned by the charming and enthusiastic owners of the site.

**Facilities:** One central, modern and well equipped toilet and block with basins in cabins and preset showers. Facilities for babies and campers with disabilities. Covered laundry and washing up area. Bar and takeaway (16/4-25/9). Fridge hire. Bicycle hire. Fishing. Wifi. Communal meals, Weekly welcoming drink. Off site: Restaurant at far side of lake. Golf 7 km. Gourdon for shopping and the Grottes de Cougnac 11 km. Sarlat for Saturday market.

**Open:** 16 April - 25 September.

**Directions:** From Sarlat on D704 go through Groléjac and at end of village turn right on to the D50 signed Domme. After 100 m. turn left, site is 500 m. on left  GPS: 44.802103, 1.294493

### Charges guide

| Per unit incl. 2 persons and electricity (6A) | € 13,00 - € 15,50 |
| --- | --- |
| extra person | € 3,50 - € 3,80 |

## You might like to know

No kill policy for pike and black bass (15 April - 15 October). Fishing permitted from 07.00 to 21.00. Max. 4 lines per angler for carp fishing. No licence or permit needed for the site lake.

☑ Coarse fishing
☐ Fly fishing
☐ Sea fishing
☑ Lake on site
☐ River on site
☐ Lake nearby (max 5 km)
☐ River nearby (max 5 km)
☐ Licence / permit required
☐ Equipment hire available
☐ Bait and fishing supplies

# Castel Camping le Ty-Nadan

Route d'Arzano, F-29310 Locunolé (Finistère)
t: 02 98 71 75 47   e: infos@camping-ty-nadan.fr
alanrogers.com/FR29010   www.camping-ty-nadan.fr

Accommodation: ☑Pitch  ☑Mobile home/chalet  ☐Hotel/B&B  ☐Apartment

Ty-Nadan is a well organised site set amongst wooded countryside along the bank of the River Elle. There are 183 grassy pitches for touring units, many with shade and 99 fully serviced. The outdoor pool with slides and paddling pool is very popular as are the large indoor pool complex and indoor games area with a climbing wall. There is also an adventure play park and a 'Minikids' park for 5-8 year olds, not to mention tennis courts, table tennis, pool tables, archery and trampolines. This is a wonderful site for families with children. Several tour operators use the site. An exciting and varied programme of activities is offered throughout the season – canoe and sea kayaking expeditions, rock climbing, mountain biking, aqua-gym, paintball, horse riding or walking – all supervised by qualified staff. A full programme of entertainment for all ages is provided in high season including concerts, Breton evenings with pig roasts, dancing, etc. (be warned, you will be actively encouraged to join in!).

**Facilities:** Two older, split-level toilet blocks are of fair quality and include washbasins in cabins and baby rooms. A newer block provides easier access for disabled visitors. Washing machines and dryers. Restaurant, takeaway, bar and well stocked shop. Heated outdoor pool (17x8 m). Indoor pool. Small river beach (unfenced). Indoor badminton and rock climbing facility. Activity and entertainment programmes (all season). Horse riding centre. Bicycle hire. Boat hire. Canoe trips. Fishing. Internet access and WiFi (charged). Off site: Beaches 20 minutes by car. Golf 12 km.

**Open:** 27 March - 2 September.

**Directions:** Make for Arzano which is northeast of Quimperlé on the Pontivy road and turn off D22 just west of village at site sign. Site is about 3 km.  GPS: 47.90468, -3.47477

**Charges guide**

| Per unit incl. 2 persons and electricity | € 20,80 - € 47,80 |
| --- | --- |
| extra person | € 4,50 - € 9,10 |
| child (2-6 yrs) | € 1,90 - € 5,60 |
| dog | € 1,90 - € 6,00 |

## You might like to know

Opportunities for both fly and coarse fishing. First class river runs through campsite with wide variety of fish including tench, bream, dace, pike, roach and trout. Fishing equipment on sale.

☑ Coarse fishing
☐ Fly fishing
☐ Sea fishing
☐ Lake on site
☑ River on site
☐ Lake nearby (max 5 km)
☐ River nearby (max 5 km)
☑ Licence / permit required
☐ Equipment hire available
☐ Bait and fishing supplies

# Castel l'Orangerie de Lanniron

Château de Lanniron, F-29336 Quimper (Finistère)
t: 02 98 90 62 02   e: camping@lanniron.com
alanrogers.com/FR29050   www.lanniron.com

**Accommodation:** ☑Pitch  ☑Mobile home/chalet  ☐ Hotel/B&B  ☐ Apartment

L'Orangerie is a beautiful and peaceful family site set in ten acres of a 17th-century, 38-hectare country estate on the banks of the Odet river, formerly the home of the Bishops of Quimper. The site has 199 grassy pitches (156 for touring units) of three types varying in size and services. They are on flat ground laid out in rows alongside access roads with shrubs and bushes providing pleasant pitches. All have electricity and 88 have three services. The original outbuildings have been attractively converted around a walled courtyard. With lovely walks within the grounds, the restaurant and the gardens are both open to the public and in spring the rhododendrons and azaleas are magnificent. The site is just to the south of Quimper and about 15 km. from the sea and beaches at Bénodet.  In addition to the golf course (9 holes) and driving range, a training bunker and pitching area have been created along with a second putting green. The Aqua-park provides in excess of 600 m² of heated water and includes balneotherapy, spa, jacuzzi, fountains, slides and games. These facilities are free of charge to campers.

## You might like to know

L'Orangerie de Lanniron is an ideal destination to discover 'Cornouaille', a very charming area rich in tourist sites, monuments, culture and folklore. Benodet's beaches are only 15 minutes away.

☑ Coarse fishing
☐ Fly fishing
☐ Sea fishing
☑ Lake on site
☑ River on site
☐ Lake nearby (max 5 km)
☐ River nearby (max 5 km)
☐ Licence / permit required
☐ Equipment hire available
☐ Bait and fishing supplies

**Facilities:** Excellent heated block in the courtyard and second modern block serving the top areas of the site. Facilities for disabled visitors and babies. Washing machines and dryers. Motorcaravan services. Shop (15/5-9/9). Gas supplies. Bar, snacks and takeaway. New restaurant (open daily). Swimming and paddling pools. Aqua-park with waterfall, balneo, spa, jacuzzi, fountains, water slides and games. Small play area. Tennis. Minigolf. Golf course (9-hole), driving range, two putting greens, training bunker and pitching area (weekly green fee package available). Fishing. Archery. Bicycle hire. TV/video room. Karaoke. Pony rides and tree climbing (high season). Internet access and WiFi. Off site: Beach 15 km.

**Open:** 15 May - 15 September.

**Directions:** From Quimper follow Quimper Sud signs, then 'Toutes Directions' and general camping signs, finally signs for Lanniron. GPS: 47.97685, -4.11102

**Charges guide**

| Per unit incl. 2 persons and electricity | € 22,00 - € 38,60 |
| --- | --- |
| extra person | € 4,30 - € 7,50 |
| child (2-9 yrs) | € 2,80 - € 4,80 |
| dog | € 2,80 - € 4,50 |

# Campéole Ile des Papes

Barrage de Villeneuve, F-30400 Villeneuve-lez-Avignon (Gard)
t: 04 90 15 15 90   e: ile-des-papes@campeole.com
alanrogers.com/FR30120   www.campeole.com

Accommodation: ☑Pitch  ☑Mobile home/chalet  ☐Hotel/B&B  ☐Apartment

Camping Ile des Papes is a large, open and very well equipped site. Avignon and its Palace and museums are 8 km. away. The site has an extensive swimming pool area and a fishing lake with beautiful mature gardens. The railway is quite near but noise is not too intrusive. The 450 pitches, 246 for touring (all with 6A electricity), are of a good size on level grass, but with little shade. Games and competitions for all ages are organised in high season. This site is very popular with groups and is especially busy at weekends and in high season. In July and August a minibus is available for transport to Avignon, the airport and the railway station; the local bus can take you directly to Avignon. A good base to explore the famous Routes des Vins and the old villages and ancient towns of the Provençal region. There are many walks and cycle routes close by.

## You might like to know

This site is situated on a small private island on the banks of the Rhone and is under an hours drive from the Mediterranean. During the summer months there are river trips to the famous Pont d'Avignon.

- ☑ Coarse fishing
- ☐ Fly fishing
- ☐ Sea fishing
- ☑ Lake on site
- ☑ River on site
- ☐ Lake nearby (max 5 km)
- ☐ River nearby (max 5 km)
- ☐ Licence / permit required
- ☐ Equipment hire available
- ☐ Bait and fishing supplies

**Facilities:** Good quality toilet blocks (may be stretched when busy) include baby rooms and facilities for campers with disabilities. Washing machines. Motorcaravan services. Well stocked shop. Bar and restaurant (1/4-20/10, limited hours in low season). Large swimming pool complex and pool for children, all unheated, (15/4-31/10). Play area. Lake for fishing. Archery, tennis, minigolf and basketball (all free). Bicycle hire. Off site: Riding 3 km. Golf 6 km. Boat launching 5 km. Parachuting, paintball, jetski. Villeneuve-lez-Avignon with shops, bars, restaurants. Avignon 6 km.

**Open:** 25 March - 20 October.

**Directions:** Leave the A9 at exit 22 for Roquemaure. Take D976 to Roquemaure, turn south D980 towards Villeneuve. Near railway bridge turn hard left, D780 (site signed). Cross river, immediately turn right to site.
GPS: 43.97660, 4.79440

**Charges guide**

| Per unit incl. 2 persons | |
|---|---|
| and electricity | € 19,10 - € 29,00 |
| extra person | € 4,50 - € 4,90 |
| child (under 7 yrs) | free - € 3,90 |
| dog | € 2,00 - € 2,90 |

# Domaine Lacs de Gascogne

Rue du Lac, F-32260 Seissan (Gers)
t: 05 62 66 27 94  e: info@domainelacsdegascogne.eu
alanrogers.com/FR32180  www.domainelacsdegascogne.eu

**Accommodation:** ☑Pitch ☑Mobile home/chalet ☑Hotel/B&B ☐Apartment

This is a spacious site located at Seissan in the Pyrénéan foothills. Its impressive drive sweeps around the largest of three lakes into the spacious and relaxing Domaine. The 25 large grassy touring pitches mostly have shade and lake views. Electricity is 16A (long leads). Comfortable chalets (25) can be rented. The attractive swimming and saltwater pools are on a creamy stone terrace, close to the sauna, gym, and new sanitary block. The bar and restaurant are open all season and the food is very good. The lakes are perfect for fishing, kayaking, and evening beach campfires. Across the lakes is ideal for 'wilder' camping, this area also has five tepees. Your friendly hosts will warmly welcome you and take time to explain all the activities, such as a tennis court, a five-a-side football pitch, archery, cycling and walking. Special theme weeks and days focus on cooking, painting and local culture. High season brings clubs for 4-16 year olds and in the evenings families can enjoy a varied programme of music and entertainment. The site is close to Auch, a beautiful city with an excellent Thursday morning market.

## You might like to know

Our restaurant is open all year serving delicious regional meals; and fishing of course is for free!

☑ Coarse fishing
☐ Fly fishing
☐ Sea fishing
☑ Lake on site
☐ River on site
☐ Lake nearby (max 5 km)
☑ River nearby (max 5 km)
☐ Licence / permit required
☐ Equipment hire available
☐ Bait and fishing supplies

**Facilities:** Excellent sanitary facilities in a new block were clean, tidy and well maintained. A second older block is across the lake. Baby changing mats and facilities for disabled visitors. Restaurant with lunch and à la carte menus. Breakfast service. Lounge. TV room. Swimming pool. Health pool. Sauna. Gym. Fishing. Kayaks. Rope raft across lake. Play area. Children's play room. Tennis court. Football. Basketball. Bicycle hire. Tourist information. Entertainment and activity programme with twice weekly music and dancing. Mobile home and bed and breakfast accommodation. Off site: Riding 5 km. Golf 6 km. Supermarket 7 km. Auch 19 km. Walking and cycle tracks.

**Open:** 15 February - 15 December.

**Directions:** Head south from Auch on N21 and, at Beaulieu, join the southbound D929. Continue on this road as far as Seissan and then follow signs to the site.  GPS: 43.49535, 0.57826

### Charges guide

| | |
|---|---|
| Per unit incl. 2 persons | € 9,00 - € 30,00 |
| extra person | € 6,00 |

# Airotel Camping de la Côte d'Argent

F-33990 Hourtin-Plage (Gironde)
t: 05 56 09 10 25  e: info@cca33.com
alanrogers.com/FR33110  www.cca33.com

Accommodation: ☑Pitch  ☑Mobile home/chalet  ☐Hotel/B&B  ☑Apartment

Côte d'Argent is a large, well equipped site for leisurely family holidays. It makes an ideal base for walkers and cyclists with over 100 kilometres of cycle lanes in the area. Hourtin-Plage is a pleasant invigorating resort on the Atlantic coast and a popular location for watersports enthusiasts. The site's top attraction is its pool complex where wooden bridges connect the pools and islands and there are sunbathing and play areas plus an indoor heated pool. The site has 588 touring pitches (all with 10A electricity), not clearly defined, arranged under trees with some on soft sand. Entertainment takes place at the bar near the entrance (until 00.30). Spread over 20 hectares of undulating sand-based terrain and in the midst of a pine forest. There are 48 hardstandings for motorcaravans outside the site, providing a cheap stopover, but with no access to site facilities. The site is well organised and ideal for children.

## You might like to know

Free fishing at the ocean beach – surf casting (300 m); or with a licence on the lake (4 km). Sea fishing boat trips can be arranged.

☐ Coarse fishing
☐ Fly fishing
☑ Sea fishing
☐ Lake on site
☐ River on site
☑ Lake nearby (max 5 km)
☐ River nearby (max 5 km)
☑ Licence / permit required
☑ Equipment hire available
☑ Bait and fishing supplies

**Facilities:** Very clean sanitary blocks include provision for disabled visitors. Washing machines. Motorcaravan service points. Large supermarket, restaurant, takeaway, pizzeria bar (all 1/6-15/9). Four outdoor pools with slides and flumes (1/6-19/9). Indoor pool (all season). Massage (Institut de Beauté). Tennis. Play areas. Miniclub, organised entertainment in season. Bicycle hire. Internet. ATM. Charcoal barbecues are not permitted. Hotel (12 rooms). Off site: Path to the beach 300 m. Fishing and riding. Golf 30 km.

**Open:** 12 May - 19 September.

**Directions:** Turn off D101 Hourtin - Soulac road 3 km. north of Hourtin. Then join D101E signed Hourtin-Plage. Site is 300 m. from the beach. GPS: 45.22297, -1.16465

### Charges guide

| Per unit incl. 2 persons and electricity | € 24,00 - € 52,00 |
|---|---|
| extra person | € 3,00 - € 7,50 |
| child (3-9 yrs) | € 2,50 - € 6,50 |
| dog | € 2,00 - € 5,50 |

# Camping le Tedey

Par le Moutchic, route de Longarisse, F-33680 Lacanau-Lac (Gironde)
t: 05 56 03 00 15   e: camping@le-tedey.com
alanrogers.com/FR33290   www.le-tedey.com

**Accommodation:** ☑Pitch  ☑Mobile home/chalet  ☐ Hotel/B&B  ☐ Apartment

With direct access to a large lake and beach, this site enjoys a beautiful tranquil position set in an area of 14 hectares amidst mature pine trees. There are 700 pitches of which 670 are for touring units, with just 30 mobile homes and chalets available for rent. The pitches are generally level and grassy although the site is on a slope. Dappled sunlight is available through the trees. Electricity is available to all pitches and 223 also have water and waste water drainage. The bar is close to the lake with a large indoor and outdoor seating area. The owners and staff are friendly and helpful and English is spoken. There is an open air cinema on Saturdays and Wednesdays as well as other entertainment in July and August. A children's club is also organised. The takeaway sells a variety of food and the shop next door is well stocked. This is an attractive well maintained site where you get a feeling of space and calm. There are many places of interest nearby and it is just a short drive to Bordeaux.

## You might like to know
On the shore of Lac Lacanau, amidst the calm of a pine forest, this is a paradise for walking, cycling and sailing – as well as fishing.

☑ Coarse fishing
☐ Fly fishing
☐ Sea fishing
☑ Lake on site
☐ River on site
☐ Lake nearby (max 5 km)
☑ River nearby (max 5 km)
☐ Licence / permit required
☐ Equipment hire available
☐ Bait and fishing supplies

**Facilities:** Four modern sanitary blocks with facilities for disabled visitors and babies. Laundry facilities. Bar with terrace. Crêperie. Takeaway. Bicycle hire. Boating on the lake. Pétanque. Playground. Gas barbecues only on pitches. Dogs are not accepted in July/Aug. Internet access. Off site: Surfing. Riding. Golf. Cycling.

**Open:** 28 April - 19 September.

**Directions:** From Lacanau take the D6 to Lacanau-Océan. Take Route de Longarisse and the campsite is well signed. GPS: 44.98620, -1.13410

### Charges guide

| Per unit incl. 1 or 2 persons and electricity | € 17,00 - € 21,00 |
| --- | --- |
| incl. water and drainage | € 21,00 - € 25,00 |
| extra person | € 3,50 - € 5,50 |
| child (2-10 yrs) | € 2,70 - € 3,20 |

# Camping le Moulin Fort

F-37150 Francueil-Chenonceau (Indre-et-Loire)
t: **02 47 23 86 22**  e: **lemoulinfort@wanadoo.fr**
alanrogers.com/FR37030  www.lemoulinfort.com

**Accommodation:** ☑Pitch  ☑Mobile home/chalet  ☐ Hotel/B&B  ☐ Apartment

Camping Le Moulin Fort is a tranquil, riverside site with British owners, John and Sarah Scarratt. The 137 pitches are enhanced by trees and shrubs offering plenty of shade and 110 pitches have electricity (6A). From the snack bar terrace adjacent to the restored mill building, a timber walkway over the mill race leads to the unheated swimming pool and paddling pools. The site is ideal for couples and families with young children, although the river is unfenced. There is occasional noise from trains passing on the opposite bank of the river. All over the campsite, visitors will find little information boards about local nature (birds, fish, trees and shrubs), about the history of the mill and fascinating facts about recycling. The owners are keen to encourage recycling on the site. The picturesque Château of Chenonceau is little more than 1 km. along the Cher riverbank and many of the Loire châteaux are within easy reach, particularly Amboise and its famous Leonardo de Vinci museum.

## You might like to know

The fortnight permit, sold in reception, also allows you to fish in other rivers and lakes in this département and is valid in 60 départements throughout west and southwest France.

☑ **Coarse fishing**
☐ **Fly fishing**
☐ **Sea fishing**
☐ **Lake on site**
☑ **River on site**
☐ **Lake nearby (max 5 km)**
☐ **River nearby (max 5 km)**
☑ **Licence / permit required**
☐ **Equipment hire available**
☐ **Bait and fishing supplies**

**Facilities:** Two toilet blocks with all the usual amenities of a good standard, include washbasins in cubicles, baby baths and facilities for disabled visitors. Motorcaravan service point. Shop, bar (limited hours), restaurant and takeaway (all 22/5-18/9). Swimming pool (22/5-18/9). Excellent play area. Minigolf. Petanque. Games room and TV. Library. Fishing. Bicycle and canoe hire. In high season regular family entertainment including wine tasting, quiz evenings, activities for children, light-hearted games tournaments and live music events. WiFi in bar area. Off site: Boat launching 2 km. River beach 4 km. Riding 12 km. Golf 20 km.

**Open:** 1 April - 30 September.

**Directions:** From A85 at exit 11 take D31 towards Bléré and turn east on D976 (Vierzon) for 7 km. then turn north on D80 (Chenonceau) to site. From north bank of Cher (D140/D40) turn south on D80 to cross river between Chenonceau and Chisseaux. Site on left just after bridge. GPS: 47.32735, 1.08936

**Charges 2011**

| Per unit incl. 2 persons and electricity | € 18,00 - € 26,00 |
| --- | --- |
| extra person | € 3,00 - € 5,00 |
| child (4-12 yrs) | € 3,00 - € 4,00 |

FRANCE – Loches-en-Touraine

# Kawan Village la Citadelle

Avenue Aristide Briand, F-37600 Loches-en-Touraine (Indre-et-Loire)
t: 02 47 59 05 91  e: camping@lacitadelle.com
alanrogers.com/FR37050  www.lacitadelle.com

Accommodation: ☑Pitch ☑Mobile home/chalet ☐ Hotel/B&B ☐ Apartment

A pleasant, well maintained site, one of La Citadelle's best features is that it is within walking distance of Loches, noted for its perfect architecture and its glorious history, yet at the same time the site has a rural atmosphere. The 86 standard touring pitches are all level, of a good size and with 10A electricity. Numerous trees offer varying degrees of shade. The 30 larger serviced pitches have 16A electricity but little shade. Mobile homes (28 for hire) occupy the other 48 pitches. Loches, with its château and historic dungeons, is a gentle 500 m. walk along the river. A free bus/little train runs from the campsite to the centre of Loches during the summer. An excellent spa centre and the municipal tennis courts are adjacent to the site and many activities are organised during July and August.

## You might like to know
Fishing permits can be bought on site, and are also available at the local tourist office.

- ☑ Coarse fishing
- ☐ Fly fishing
- ☐ Sea fishing
- ☐ Lake on site
- ☑ River on site
- ☐ Lake nearby (max 5 km)
- ☐ River nearby (max 5 km)
- ☑ Licence / permit required
- ☐ Equipment hire available
- ☐ Bait and fishing supplies

**Facilities:** Three sanitary blocks provide mainly British style WCs, washbasins (mostly in cabins) and controllable showers. The block at the 'shady' end could be under pressure in high season. Laundry facilities. Motorcaravan service point. Two baby units and provision for disabled visitors. Heated swimming pool (May-Sept). Paddling pool and play area (adult supervision strongly recommended). Small bar and snack bar (15/6-15/9). Boules. Games room. Internet access and TV. Fishing. Off site: Supermarket, station and buses within 1 km. Bicycle hire 50 m. Riding 5 km. Golf and river beach both 10 km. Large market in Loches on Wednesday and Saturday mornings.

**Open:** 19 March - 10 October.

**Directions:** Loches is 45 km. southeast of Tours. Site is well signed from most directions. Do not enter town centre. Approach from roundabout by supermarket at southern end of bypass (D943). Site signed towards town centre and is on right in 800 m.  GPS: 47.12303, 1.00223

## Charges guide

| Per unit incl. 2 persons and electricity | € 19,50 - € 29,00 |
|---|---|

54

# Camping les Coteaux du Lac

Base de Loisirs, F-37460 Chemillé-sur-Indrois (Indre-et-Loire)
t: 02 47 92 77 83  e: lescoteauxdulac@wanadoo.fr
alanrogers.com/FR37150  www.lescoteauxdulac.com

**Accommodation:** ☑Pitch  ☑Mobile home/chalet  ☐ Hotel/B&B  ☐ Apartment

This former municipal site has been completely refurbished to a high standard and is being operated efficiently by a private company owned by the present enthusiastic manager, Thiery Licois. There are 49 touring pitches, all with electricity (10A) and individual water tap; four have hardstanding for motorcaravans. At present there is little shade apart from that offered by a few mature trees, but new trees and bushes have been planted and flower beds are to be added. In a few years this promises to be a delightful site; meanwhile it is smart and very well tended. The site is in pleasant countryside above a lake and next to a rapidly developing Base de Loisirs with watersports provision and a bar/restaurant. There is a good, well-equipped little swimming pool with a paddling area securely separated from the main pool. The site is near the town of Loches which has an attractive château, and is an easy drive to Tours and the many châteaux along the Loire and the Indre.

## You might like to know

The village's Base de Loisirs extends over 75 hectares, of which 35 are taken up by the lake.

☑ Coarse fishing
☐ Fly fishing
☐ Sea fishing
☑ Lake on site
☐ River on site
☐ Lake nearby (max 5 km)
☑ River nearby (max 5 km)
☑ Licence / permit required
☐ Equipment hire available
☐ Bait and fishing supplies

**Facilities:** Excellent sanitary block with controllable showers, some washbasins in cabins and en-suite facilities for disabled visitors. Laundry facilities. Reception sells a few basic supplies and bread can be ordered. Swimming and paddling pools. Playing field. Play equipment for different ages. Chalets to rent (15) are grouped at far end of site, Off site: Fishing 100 m. Lakeside beach, sailing and other water sports 200 m. Riding 4 km. Golf 15 km.

**Open:** 1 May - 30 September.

**Directions:** Chemillé-sur-Indrois is 55 km. southeast of Tours and 14 km. east of Loches, just off the D760 from Loches to Montrésor. Site is to the north of this road and is signed just west of Montrésor.  GPS: 47.15786, 1.15986

**Charges guide**

| Per unit incl. 2 persons | € 13,30 - € 18,30 |
| --- | --- |
| extra person | € 3,90 - € 5,00 |
| child (2-9 yrs) | € 2,20 - € 3,40 |
| electricity | € 3,90 |

# Sunêlia le Col-Vert

Lac de Léon, F-40560 Vielle-Saint-Girons (Landes)
t: **0890 710 001**  e: **contact@colvert.com**
alanrogers.com/FR40050  www.colvert.com

**Accommodation:** ☑ Pitch  ☑ Mobile home/chalet  ☐ Hotel/B&B  ☐ Apartment

This large, well maintained campsite is well laid out on the shores of Lac de Léon and offers 185 mobile homes for rent and 380 touring pitches. The pitches range from simple ones to those with water and a drain, and there are 8 with private, well designed, modern sanitary facilities. In low season it is a quiet site and those pitches beside the lake offer a wonderful backdrop to relaxing pastimes. During the main season it is a lively place for children of all ages. A pool complex offers a standard pool for swimming, a pool for children with water canon and fountains, plenty of sunbeds and a heated indoor pool. Swimming is also permitted in the lake alongside the many water-based activities. A fitness and beauty spa offers a wide range of treatments. This extensive but natural site edges a nature reserve and stretches along the Lac de Léon, a conservation area, for 1 km. on a narrow frontage. This makes it particularly suitable for those who want to practise watersports such as sailing and windsurfing. An overall charge is made for some but not all of the leisure activities.

## You might like to know

Fishing classes for children during high season (July and August), and regular fishing competitions.

☑ Coarse fishing
☐ Fly fishing
☐ Sea fishing
☑ Lake on site
☐ River on site
☐ Lake nearby (max 5 km)
☑ River nearby (max 5 km)
☑ Licence / permit required
☑ Equipment hire available
☑ Bait and fishing supplies

**Facilities:** Four toilet blocks, one heated. One block with fun facilities for children based on Disney characters. Facilities for disabled visitors. Laundry facilities. Motorcaravan services. Shops, bar/restaurant, takeaway (1/4-5/9). Swimming pool complex with three pools. Spa, fitness centre and sauna. Play area. Games room. Sports areas. Boules. Tennis. Bicycle hire. Minigolf. Fishing. Sailing school (15/6-15/9). Riding. Communal barbecues. Internet access and WiFi. Off site: Walking and cycle ways in the forest. Atlantic beaches 5 km. Golf 10 km.

**Open:** 1 April - 19 September.

**Directions:** Site is off D652 Mimizan - Léon road, 4 km. south of crossroads with D42 at St Girons. The road to the lake and the site is signed at Vielle.  GPS: 43.90285, -1.3125

### Charges guide

| Per unit incl. 2 persons and electricity | € 14,20 - € 53,80 |
| --- | --- |
| extra person | € 2,00 - € 6,50 |
| child (3-13 yrs) | € 1,50 - € 5,50 |
| dog | € 1,00 - € 4,30 |

FRANCE – Mimizan-Plage

# Airotel Club Marina-Landes

Rue Marina, F-40200 Mimizan (Landes)
t: 05 58 09 12 66  e: contact@clubmarina.com
alanrogers.com/FR40080  www.marinalandes.com

Accommodation: ☑Pitch ☑Mobile home/chalet ☐Hotel/B&B ☐Apartment

Well maintained and clean, with helpful staff, Club Marina-Landes would be a very good choice for a family holiday. Activities include discos, play groups for children, specially trained staff to entertain teenagers and concerts for more mature campers. There are numerous sports opportunities and a superb sandy beach nearby. A nightly curfew ensures that all have a good night's sleep. The site has 443 touring pitches (333 with 10A electricity) and 128 mobile homes and chalets for rent. The pitches are on firm grass, most with hedges and they are large (mostly 100 m² or larger). If ever a campsite could be said to have two separate identities, then Club Marina-Landes is surely the one. In early and late season it is quiet, with the pace of life in low gear – come July and until 1st September, all the facilities are open and there is fun for all the family with the chance that family members will only meet together at meal times.

## You might like to know

Why not take the Mailloueyre lake trail (1 km – 15 minutes on foot)? The area is classified as a natural reserve – a delight for botany fans and nature lovers.

- ☑ Coarse fishing
- ☐ Fly fishing
- ☐ Sea fishing
- ☐ Lake on site
- ☐ River on site
- ☑ Lake nearby (max 5 km)
- ☑ River nearby (max 5 km)
- ☑ Licence / permit required
- ☐ Equipment hire available
- ☑ Bait and fishing supplies

**Facilities:** Five toilet blocks (opened as required), well maintained with showers and many washbasins in cabins. Facilities for babies, children and disabled visitors. Laundry facilities. Motorcaravan services. Fridge hire. Shop (freshly baked bread) and bar (May-9/9). Restaurant, snack bar, pizzas and takeaway (May-9/9). Covered pool and outdoor pools (May-12/9). Minigolf. Tennis. Bicycle hire. Play area. Internet access. Entertainment and activities (high season). Gas or electric barbecues only.
Off site: Beach and fishing 500 m. Bus service 1 km. Riding 1 km. Golf 8 km. Mimizan 8 km.

**Open:** 30 April - 13 September.

**Directions:** Heading west from Mimizan centre, take D626 passing Abbey Museum. Straight on at lights (crossing D87/D67). Next lights turn left. After 2 km. at T-junction turn left. Follow signs to site.  GPS: 44.20447, -1.29099

### Charges guide

| Per unit incl. 3 persons and electricity | € 18,00 - € 49,00 |
|---|---|
| extra person | € 3,00 - € 8,00 |
| child (3-13 yrs) | € 3,00 - € 6,00 |
| dog | € 2,00 - € 5,00 |

# Kawan Village du Deffay

B.P. 18 Le Deffay, Sainte Reine-de-Bretagne, F-44160 Pontchâteau (Loire-Atlantique)
t: 02 40 88 00 57   e: campingdudeffay@wanadoo.fr
alanrogers.com/FR44090   www.camping-le-deffay.com

Accommodation: ☑Pitch  ☑Mobile home/chalet  ☑Hotel/B&B  ☐ Apartment

A family managed site, Château du Deffay is a refreshing departure from the usual formula in that it is not over organised or supervised and has no tour operator units. The 142 good sized, fairly level pitches have pleasant views and are either on open grass, on shallow terraces divided by hedges, or informally arranged in a central, slightly sloping wooded area. Most have electricity. The facilities are located within the old courtyard area of the smaller château that dates from before 1400. A significant attraction of the site is the large, unfenced lake which is well stocked for fishermen and even has free pedaloes for children. The landscape is wonderfully natural and the site blends well with the rural environment of the estate, lake and farmland which surround it. Alpine type chalets overlook the lake and the larger château (built 1880 and which now offers B&B) stands slightly away from the camping area but provides a wonderful backdrop for an evening stroll. The site is close to the Brière Regional Park, the Guérande Peninsula, and La Baule and is just 20 minutes drive from the nearest beach.

**Facilities:** The main toilet block is well maintained, if a little dated and is well equipped including washbasins in cabins, provision for disabled visitors and a baby bathroom. Laundry facilities. Shop, bar, small restaurant with takeaway (1/5-20/9). Covered and heated swimming pool (at 28 degrees when we visited) and paddling pool (all season). Play area. TV. Animation in season including miniclub. Torches useful. Off site: Golf 7 km. Riding 10 km. Beach 25 km.

**Open:** 1 May - 30 September.

**Directions:** Site is signed from D33 Pontchâteau - Herbignac road near Sainte Reine. Also signed from the D773 and N165-E60 (exit 13). GPS: 47.44106, -2.15981

**Charges guide**

| Per unit incl. 2 persons and electricity | € 18,10 - € 27,80 |
| --- | --- |
| extra person | € 3,30 - € 5,50 |
| child (2-12 yrs) | € 2,30 - € 3,80 |

## Special offers
Fishing on the campsite lake is free of charge.

☑ Coarse fishing
☐ Fly fishing
☐ Sea fishing
☑ Lake on site
☐ River on site
☐ Lake nearby (max 5 km)
☐ River nearby (max 5 km)
☐ Licence / permit required
☐ Equipment hire available
☐ Bait and fishing supplies

## You might like to know
A no kill policy is applied. Fish here include roach, rudd, zander, eel and catfish.

# Camping Hortus, l'Ile du Château

Avenue de la Boire Salée, F-49130 Les Ponts-de-Cé (Maine-et-Loire)

t: **02 38 36 35 94**  e: **info@camping-hortus.com**

alanrogers.com/FR49110  www.camping-hortus.com

Accommodation: ☑Pitch  ☑Mobile home/chalet  ☐ Hotel/B&B  ☐ Apartment

This could be a very useful site for those wishing to visit Angers and tour the surrounding vineyards and châteaux from a no-nonsense campsite offering good value for money. Just five kilometres from the city centre, the site is on an island in the Loire, though sadly one arm of the river is now dry in summer because of reservoirs upstream. A camping field (25 pitches without electricity) overlooks this, while the main area has 89 touring pitches on generally level ground, with lots of mature trees offering shade, separated by hedges and all with electricity (6A). It is well tended by its friendly managers who are keen to welcome more British visitors.

## You might like to know

The Loire remains one of Europes last wild rivers, passing through the heart of Angers. Ponts-de-Cé is a string of islands, which have been shaped by the river, boasting some fine medieval architecture.

☑ Coarse fishing
☐ Fly fishing
☐ Sea fishing
☐ Lake on site
☑ River on site
☐ Lake nearby (max 5 km)
☐ River nearby (max 5 km)
☑ Licence / permit required
☐ Equipment hire available
☐ Bait and fishing supplies

**Facilities:** The main sanitary block is traditional, kept clean and offers reasonable provision. Mainly seatless WCs, with some Turkish. Facilities for disabled visitors. Baby bath. Laundry facilities. Motorcaravan service point. Small shop selling basics (bread can be ordered). Simple, open air bar with snacks and takeaway (all 1/7-31/8). Boules. Bicycle hire. Adjacent open-air leisure pool. WiFi. Security barrier. Off site: Takeaway pizza, bus stop, fishing, canoe/kayak hire, all 200 m. Riding 2 km. Golf 7 km. Supermarket, bars and restaurant nearby.

**Open:** 7 April - 31 October.

**Directions:** Les Ponts-de-Cé is just off the N260 Angers eastern bypass. Take exit west onto D4 signed Ponts-de-Cé and Bouchemaine. In 1.5 km. turn south on N160 signed to town centre and campsite. After about 1 km. turn right at post office, next to a small roundabout into campsite road. Road is narrow and may be difficult for large units. Do not use satnav on final approach. GPS: 47.424583, -0.5291

### Charges guide

| | |
|---|---|
| Per unit incl. 2 persons | € 15,00 - € 20,00 |
| extra person | € 3,00 - € 4,00 |
| dog | € 2,00 |

# Camping Parc de Vaux

35 rue des Colverts, F-53300 Ambrières-les-Vallées (Mayenne)

t: 02 43 04 90 25   e: parcdevaux@camp-in-ouest.com

alanrogers.com/FR53010   www.parcdevaux.com

**Accommodation:** ☑Pitch  ☑Mobile home/chalet  ☐ Hotel/B&B  ☐ Apartment

Parc de Vaux is an ex-municipal site which was acquired in 2010 by new owners. This 3.5 hectare site has 90 pitches, 18 occupied by mobile homes, chalets and bungalow tents, available to rent. The 59 touring pitches are generally grassy and well sized (most with 10A electricity and water). The site is close to the pretty village of Ambrières-les-Vallées, and there is direct access to the village from the site by a footbridge over the river. The village is around 12 km. north of Mayenne, and may prove a convenient en-route stop. There is a swimming pool adjacent (with water slide) and the site also has access to a lake and a good range of amenities. Parc de Vaux is adjacent to the River Varenne which runs into the Mayenne. This river was the region's most important transport artery for many years, dating back to the times of Charlemagne. It is now an important tourist feature with a great many pleasure craft in the summer. Ambrières-les-Vallées is now an attractive riverside resort with many cafes and restaurants, as well as its interesting Musée des Tisserands.

## You might like to know

Night fishing for carp is permitted here.

☑ **Coarse fishing**
☐ **Fly fishing**
☐ **Sea fishing**
☐ **Lake on site**
☑ **River on site**
☑ **Lake nearby (max 5 km)**
☐ **River nearby (max 5 km)**
☑ **Licence / permit required**
☐ **Equipment hire available**
☐ **Bait and fishing supplies**

**Facilities:** Three small toilet blocks, one with facilities for disabled visitors. No children's facilities. Laundry. Motorcaravan service point. Bar and snack bar/takeaway in high season. Heated outdoor swimming pool. Sports field. Fishing. Football. Basketball. Minigolf. Boules. Canoes. Pedaloes. Bicycle hire. Archery and tennis adjacent. Games room with TV and library. Play area. Mobile homes, chalets and bungalow tents for rent. Off site: Ambrières-les-Vallées (shops and restaurants). Boating on the River Mayenne. Walking and cycle tracks.

**Open:** 1 April - 1 November.

**Directions:** From Mayenne head north on the D23 to Ambrières-les-Vallées. The site is clearly signed on your right-hand side from from here. GPS: 48.391908, -0.61709

### Charges guide

| | |
|---|---|
| Per unit incl. 2 persons | € 10,40 - € 12,90 |
| extra person | € 3,20 - € 4,20 |
| child (under 13 yrs) | € 1,70 - € 2,30 |
| electricity | € 3,10 |
| animal | € 1,30 - € 1,80 |

FRANCE – Bassemberg

# Campéole le Giessen

Route de Villé, F-67220 Bassemberg (Bas-Rhin)
t: 03 88 58 98 14  e: giessen@campeole.com
alanrogers.com/FR67070  www.campeole.com

Accommodation: ☑Pitch ☑Mobile home/chalet ☐ Hotel/B&B ☐ Apartment

Le Giessen is a member of the Campéole group and can be found at the foot of the Vosges mountains, with easy access to many of the best loved sights in Alsace. Although there is no pool on site, a large complex, comprising an indoor and outdoor pool with a water slide, can be found adjacent to the site, with free admission for all campers. Pitches here are grassy and of a good size, mostly with electrical connections. A number of mobile homes and fully equipped tents are available for rent. Various activities are organised in high season including a children's club and disco evenings. Nearby places of interest include the magnificent fortified castle of Haut-Koenigsbourg, as well as the great cities of Strasbourg and Colmar. This is a good base for exploring the Vosges and the Route du Vin (bicycle hire in the village). The site's friendly managers will be pleased to recommend possible itineraries.

**Facilities:** Multisport court. Bar. Play area. Activities and entertainment. Tourist information. Mobile homes and equipped tents for rent. Off site: Swimming pool complex adjacent. Tennis. Rollerblading rink. Hiking and mountain biking. Bicycle hire. Riding. Strasbourg 50 km.

**Open:** 1 April - 18 September.

**Directions:** Leave A35 autoroute at exit 17 (Villé) and follow the D697 to Villé. Continue south on D39 to Bassemberg from where the site is well indicated.  GPS: 48.33722, 7.28862

**Charges guide**

Per unit incl. 2 persons
and electricity                    € 15,10 - € 24,50

## You might like to know
Access to the neighbouring watersports centre is free and unlimited (closes for 4 days at Easter and the first week in September).

☑ Coarse fishing
☐ Fly fishing
☐ Sea fishing
☐ Lake on site
☑ River on site
☐ Lake nearby (max 5 km)
☐ River nearby (max 5 km)
☐ Licence / permit required
☐ Equipment hire available
☐ Bait and fishing supplies

# Kawan Village Château de l'Epervière

F-71240 Gigny-sur-Saône (Saône-et-Loire)

t: **03 85 94 16 90**   e: **domaine-de-leperviere@wanadoo.fr**

alanrogers.com/FR71070   www.domaine-eperviere.com

**Accommodation:** ☑Pitch  ☑Mobile home/chalet  ☐ Hotel/B&B  ☐ Apartment

This popular and high quality site is peacefully situated in the wooded grounds of a 16th-century château, close to the A6 and near the village of Gigny-sur-Saône. It is within walking distance of the river where you can watch the cruise boats on their way to and from Châlon-sur-Saône. There are 160 pitches in two separate areas, of which 100 are used for touring, all with 10A electricity. Some are on hard standing and 30 are fully serviced. Some pitches, close to the château and fishing lake, are hedged and have shade from mature trees. The other area has a more open aspect. Red squirrels, ducks and the occasional heron can be found on the campsite and the pitches around the periphery are good for birdwatchers. The château's main restaurant serves regional dishes and there is a good range of takeaway meals. Gert-Jan, François and their team enthusiastically organise many activities, mainly for children, but including wine tasting in the cellars of the château. Don't forget, here you are in the Maconnais and Châlonnaise wine regions, so arrange some visits to the local caves.

## Special offers

Special low season offer: Camping Cheques accepted.

## You might like to know

Free fishing in the 1.5 ha. lake on site, great for carp. Permit required for fishing in the River Saône, only 500 yards from the campsite.

☑ Coarse fishing
☐ Fly fishing
☐ Sea fishing
☑ Lake on site
☐ River on site
☐ Lake nearby (max 5 km)
☑ River nearby (max 5 km)
☐ Licence / permit required
☐ Equipment hire available
☑ Bait and fishing supplies

**Facilities:** Two well equipped, very clean toilet blocks with all necessary facilities including those for babies and campers with disabilities. Washing machine/dryer. Basic shop (1/5-30/9). Restaurant with good menu and takeaway (1/4-30/9). Cellar with wine tasting. Converted barn with bar. Unheated outdoor pool (1/5-30/9) partly enclosed by old stone walls. Smaller indoor heated pool, jacuzzi, sauna (1/4-30/9). Play areas with paddling pool. Fishing. Bicycle hire. Motorcaravan services. WiFi. Off site: Boat launching 500 m. Riding 15 km. Golf 20 km. Historic towns of Châlon and Tournus, both 20 km. The Monday market of Louhans, to see the famous Bresse chickens 26 km.

**Open:** 1 April - 30 September.

**Directions:** From A6 heading south, take exit 26 Châlon-Sud, or from A6 heading north take exit 27 Tournus. Then N6 to Sennecey-le-Grand, turn east D18, signed Gigny. Follow site signs to site (6.5 km). GPS: 46.65485, 4.94463

## Charges guide

| Per unit incl. 2 persons and electricity | € 23,40 - € 33,50 |
| --- | --- |
| extra person | € 5,70 - € 8,10 |
| child (under 7 yrs) | € 3,50 - € 5,60 |
| dog | € 2,40 - € 3,00 |

FRANCE – Marçon

# Camping Lac des Varennes

Saint Lezin, route de Port-Gauthier, F-72340 Marçon (Sarthe)
t: 02 43 44 13 72  e: lacdesvarennes@camp-in-ouest.com
alanrogers.com/FR72080  www.lacdesvarennes.com

Accommodation: ☑Pitch ☑Mobile home/chalet ☐Hotel/B&B ☐Apartment

This extensive site is located near the massive forest of Bercé in the Vallée du Loir, and is on the shore of the lake from which it takes its name. There are 250 pitches here, with 175 for tourers, all grassy and with electrical connections (10A). Many also have lake views. The site has its own sandy beach (with a beach volleyball court) and canoes are available for rent. In high season, various activities are organised including a club for children and riding. Mobile homes are available for rent. A gate gives free access to the Base de Loisirs which offers a variety of water and land-based activities. The area is a paradise for walkers and cyclists, with more than 300 km. of tracks through the Forêt de Bercé; the site owners will be pleased to recommend routes. Nearby are the vineyards of Côteaux de Loir whilst the nearest point on the River Loire is just 50 km. to the south, so visits to some of its famous châteaux are possible.

## You might like to know
The lake here is well known for its record breaking carp catches. Marçon is however also well known for its green landscapes, rich gastronomy and famous wines.

- ☑ Coarse fishing
- ☐ Fly fishing
- ☐ Sea fishing
- ☑ Lake on site
- ☐ River on site
- ☐ Lake nearby (max 5 km)
- ☐ River nearby (max 5 km)
- ☐ Licence / permit required
- ☐ Equipment hire available
- ☐ Bait and fishing supplies

**Facilities:** Three traditional sanitary blocks are kept clean and provide pushbutton showers, some washbasins in cubicles and a mix of British and Turkish-style toilets. Washing machines and dryer. Basic facilities for disabled visitors. Motorcaravan service point. Shop, snack bar and takeaway (July/Aug). Simple bar with games and TV. Play area. Motorcaravan services. Organised entertainment (July/Aug). Direct access to lake with fishing and swimming. Off site: Base de Loisirs with sailing, boat launching, water slide, carp fishing, tennis, plus (weekends and July/Aug) pedaloes and archery. Riding 5 km. Walking and cycling in the forest 8 km.

**Open:** 27 March - 12 November.

**Directions:** Marçon is 50 km. southeast of Le Mans. From A28 exit 26, head east to Château du Loir, turn south on the D938/D338 (Caen-Tours road) and cross the Loir. Then head northeast on the D305 to Marçon, and turn west in village centre to Base de Loisirs and site on right in 1 km.  GPS: 47.7125, 0.4993

### Charges guide

| Per unit incl. 2 persons and electricity | € 13,60 - € 17,10 |
|---|---|
| extra person | € 3,50 - € 4,70 |
| child (under 13 yrs) | € 1,70 - € 2,30 |

# Campéole la Nublière

30 allée de la Nublière, F-74210 Doussard (Haute-Savoie)
t: **04 50 44 33 44**  e: **nubliere@wanadoo.fr**
alanrogers.com/FR74190  www.campeole.com

**Accommodation:** ☑Pitch ☑Mobile home/chalet ☐ Hotel/B&B ☐ Apartment

If you are looking for large pitches, shady trees, mountain views and direct access to a lakeside beach, this site is for you. There are 271 touring pitches of which 243 have electrical hook-ups (6A). This area is very popular and the site is very likely to be busy in high season. There may be some noise from the road and the public beach. La Nublière is 16 km. from old Annecy and you are spoilt for choice in how to get there. Take a ferry trip, hire a sailing boat or pedalo, or walk or cycle along the traffic free track towards the town. The local beach and sailing club are close and there is a good restaurant on the site perimeter. Across the road from the site are courts for tennis and boules. The site is perfect for walking, cycling or sailing and in low season provides a tranquil base for those just wishing to relax in natural surroundings on the edge of a nature reserve.

## You might like to know

Geneva and the Swiss border are less than an hours drive away – Geneva is a beautiful city with a stunning mountain backdrop and world famous lake shore.

- ☑ **Coarse fishing**
- ☐ **Fly fishing**
- ☐ **Sea fishing**
- ☑ **Lake on site**
- ☐ **River on site**
- ☐ **Lake nearby (max 5 km)**
- ☐ **River nearby (max 5 km)**
- ☐ **Licence / permit required**
- ☐ **Equipment hire available**
- ☐ **Bait and fishing supplies**

**Facilities:** Large clean sanitary blocks include free hot showers and good facilities for disabled visitors. Laundry. Shop (1/5-15/9). Restaurant on site perimeter (closed Mondays). Children's club (3/7-26/8) for 4-8 yrs. Safe deposit. Off site: Small supermarket adjacent to site. Good watersports area within 70 m. Access to town beach from site. Fishing 100 m. Golf and riding 4 km. Bicycle hire 7 km.

**Open:** 28 April - 18 September.

**Directions:** Site is 16 km. south of Annecy on Route d'Albertville, well signed.
GPS: 45.7908, 6.2197

**Charges guide**

| Per unit incl. 2 persons and electricity | € 17,10 - € 26,60 |
| --- | --- |
| extra person | € 4,50 - € 6,80 |
| child (2-6 yrs) | free - € 4,30 |

# Caravaning l'Etoile d'Argens

F-83370 Saint Aygulf (Var)
t: 04 94 81 01 41   e: info@etoiledargens.com
alanrogers.com/FR83070   www.etoiledargens.com

Accommodation: ☑Pitch  ☑Mobile home/chalet  ☐ Hotel/B&B  ☐ Apartment

First impressions of l'Etoile d'Argens are of space, cleanliness and calm. This is a site run with families in mind and many of the activities are free, making it an excellent choice for a good value holiday. There are 450 level, fully serviced grass pitches (all with 10/16A electricity). Separated by hedges, they range in size from 100-250 m² and mainly have good shade. The pool and bar area is attractively landscaped with olive and palm trees on beautifully kept grass. There are two heated pools (one for adults, one for children) both of which are designed very much with families in mind. Reception staff are very friendly and English is spoken. The exceptionally large pitches could easily take two caravans and cars or one family could have a very spacious plot with a garden like atmosphere. The river runs alongside the site with a free boat service to the beach (15/6-15/9). This is a good family site for the summer but also ideal in low season for a quiet stay in a superb location with excellent pitches. There are 88 mobile homes for rent. For a large site, l'Etoile d'Argens is unusually calm and peaceful, even in July.

## You might like to know

The Argens extends for 116 km through the Var, passing through such towns as Vidauban, Le Muy and Roquebrune before reaching the sea at Fréjus.

☑ **Coarse fishing**
☐ **Fly fishing**
☐ **Sea fishing**
☐ **Lake on site**
☑ **River on site**
☐ **Lake nearby (max 5 km)**
☐ **River nearby (max 5 km)**
☑ **Licence / permit required**
☐ **Equipment hire available**
☐ **Bait and fishing supplies**

**Facilities:** Over 20, well kept, small toilet blocks. Supermarket and gas supplies. Bar, restaurant, pizzeria, takeaway. Two pools (heated 1/4-30/6), paddling pool, jacuzzi, solarium. Floodlit tennis with coaching. Minigolf. Aerobics. Archery (July/Aug). Football and swimming lessons. Boules. Good play area. Children's entertainment (July/Aug). Activity programme with games, dances and escorted walking trips to the surrounding hills within 3 km. Off site: Golf and riding 2 km. Beach 3.5 km.

**Open:** 1 April - 30 September (with all services).

**Directions:** From A8 exit 36, take N7 towards Le Muy and Fréjus. After 8 km. at roundabout take D7 signed Roquebrune and St Aygulf. In 9.5 km. (after roundabout) turn left signed Fréjus. Site is signed. Ignore width and height limit signs as site is before the limit (500 m). GPS: 43.41581, 6.70545

### Charges guide

| Per unit incl. 2 persons and electricity | € 14,00 - € 38,00 |
|---|---|
| incl. 3 persons, water and drainage | € 29,00 - € 62,00 |
| luxury pitch incl. 4 persons | € 33,00 - € 72,00 |
| extra person | € 6,00 - € 9,00 |
| child (under 7 yrs) | € 5,00 - € 7,00 |

# Kawan Village les Pêcheurs

F-83520 Roquebrune-sur-Argens (Var)
t: 04 94 45 71 25  e: info@camping-les-pecheurs.com
alanrogers.com/FR83200  www.camping-les-pecheurs.com

Accommodation: ☑Pitch ☑Mobile home/chalet ☐ Hotel/B&B ☐ Apartment

Les Pêcheurs will appeal to families who appreciate natural surroundings together with many activities, cultural and sporting. Interspersed with mobile homes, the 150 good sized touring pitches (6/10A electricity) are separated by trees or flowering bushes. The Provençal style buildings are delightful, especially the bar, restaurant and games room, with its terrace down to the river and the site's own canoe station (locked gate). Across the road is a lake used exclusively for water skiing with a sandy beach, a restaurant and minigolf. Enlarged spa facilities include swimming pool, large jacuzzi, massage, steam pool and a sauna. Developed over three generations by the Simoncini family, this peaceful, friendly site is set in more than four hectares of mature, well shaded countryside at the foot of the Roquebrune Rock. Activities include climbing the 'Rock' with a guide. We became intrigued with stories about the Rock, and the Holy Hole, the Three Crosses and the Hermit all call for further exploration which reception staff are happy to arrange. The medieval village of Roquebrune is within walking distance.

## You might like to know

This site is within easy reach of the sandy beaches on the Côte d'Azur and there are three trout lakes situated less than 7 km. from the campsite.

☑ Coarse fishing
☐ Fly fishing
☐ Sea fishing
☑ Lake on site
☑ River on site
☐ Lake nearby (max 5 km)
☐ River nearby (max 5 km)
☑ Licence / permit required
☐ Equipment hire available
☐ Bait and fishing supplies

**Facilities:** Modern, refurbished, well designed toilet blocks, baby baths, facilities for disabled visitors. Washing machines. Shop. Bar and restaurant (all open all season). Heated outdoor swimming pool (all season), separate paddling pool (lifeguard in high season), ice cream bar. Games room. Spa facilities. Playing field. Fishing. Canoeing. Waterskiing. Rafting and diving schools. Activities for children and adults (high season), visits to local wine caves. Only gas or electric barbecues. WiFi in reception, bar/restaurant and pool area. Off site: Bicycle hire 1 km. Riding 5 km. Golf 5 km. (reduced fees).

**Open:** 1 April - 30 September.

**Directions:** From A8 take Le Muy exit, follow the N7 towards Fréjus for 13 km. bypassing Le Muy. After crossing A8, turn right at roundabout towards Roquebrune-sur-Argens. Site is on left after 1 km. just before bridge over river. GPS: 43.450783, 6.6335

### Charges guide

| Per unit incl. 2 persons and electricity | € 23,00 - € 43,00 |
|---|---|
| extra person | € 4,00 - € 7,80 |
| child (5-10 yrs) | € 3,20 - € 6,20 |
| dog (max. 1) | € 3,20 |

# Castel Camping la Garangeoire

F-85150 Saint Julien-des-Landes (Vendée)
t: 02 51 46 65 39   e: info@garangeoire.com
alanrogers.com/FR85040   www.camping-la-garangeoire.com

Accommodation: ☑Pitch ☑Mobile home/chalet ☐ Hotel/B&B ☐ Apartment

La Garangeoire is a stunning campsite, situated some 15 km. inland near the village of Saint Julien-des-Landes. Set in 200 ha. of parkland surrounding the small château of La Garangeoire, of which there is an outstanding view as you approach through the gates. With a spacious, relaxed atmosphere, the main camping areas are on either side of the old road which is edged with mature trees. The 360 pitches, all named after birds, are individually hedged, some with shade. They are well spaced and are especially large (most 150-200 m²), most with electricity (8A) and some with water and drainage also. Access is good for large units. Tour operators use 144 pitches. The parkland provides peaceful fields and woods for walking and three lakes, one of which is used for fishing and boating (life jackets are provided). The site is now run by the third generation of owners since 1964, Ann and Eric Bourgon.

## Special offers
Free fishing in the estate's three lakes (from 3 to 8.5 acres).

## You might like to know
Fishing instruction available on site. Weekly fishing contests. Fishing subject to licence on the Lac de Jaunay (2 km). Sea fishing at Les Sables d'Olonne (27 km).

☑ Coarse fishing
☐ Fly fishing
☑ Sea fishing
☑ Lake on site
☐ River on site
☑ Lake nearby (max 5 km)
☑ River nearby (max 5 km)
☑ Licence / permit required
☑ Equipment hire available
☑ Bait and fishing supplies

**Facilities:** Ample, first class sanitary facilities. All have washbasins in cabins. Facilities for babies and disabled visitors. Laundry facilities. Motorcaravan service point. Shop, full restaurant and takeaway (10/5-22/9) with bars and terrace (all season). Pool complex with water slides, fountains and a children's pool (all season). Play field with play equipment. Games room. Tennis courts. Bicycle hire. Minigolf. Archery. Riding (July/Aug). Fishing and boating. Bouncy castle. Six trampolines. Quadricycles (on payment). Off site: Golf 10 km. Beaches 15 km.

**Open:** 24 April - 25 September.

**Directions:** Site is signed from Saint Julien; entrance is to the east off the D21 road, 2.5 km. north of Saint Julien-des-Landes.
GPS: 46.66387, -1.71346

### Charges guide

| Per unit incl. 2 persons | |
|---|---|
| and electricity | € 17,50 - € 36,50 |
| incl. services | € 19,50 - € 39,00 |
| extra person | € 4,50 - € 7,80 |
| child (under 10 yrs) | € 2,50 - € 3,60 |
| dog | € 3,00 - € 3,50 |

# RCN Camping la Ferme du Latois

Le Latoi, F-85220 Coëx (Vendée)
t: **02 51 54 67 30**  e: **info@rcn-lafermedulatois.fr**
alanrogers.com/FR85770  www.rcn-campings.fr

**Accommodation:** ☑ Pitch  ☑ Mobile home/chalet  ☐ Hotel/B&B  ☐ Apartment

Originally a simple 'camping à la ferme', this site has been developed by a Dutch organisation into an extensive, very well equipped and well maintained campsite. Naturally a very high proportion of its clientèle is Dutch, but the owners maintain a very French ambience and are keen to attract more British visitors. Located round two attractive fishing lakes, the 199 pitches, most available for touring, are spacious and attractively laid out with plenty of grass, hedges and trees, some young, some mature. All have electricity and a few are very large. There are 22 mobile homes for rent. An old barn has been converted into a large restaurant offering an extensive French menu, including a 'menu du jour'. Also here are a small bar, a shop selling basic provisions and the reception area. Nearby is a smaller, open-ended barn that has been fitted out for actvities and has a large television to screen key events and football matches. There is a good heated pool with a paddling pool, water slides and a long flume. The busy fishing port of Saint Gilles Croix-de-Vie is just a short drive away.

## Special offers
Special camping offer: 9/4-5/7: 20% discount on your stay (minimum 7 nights). Do you prefer a mobile home or chalet? From 7-28/5, 25/6-9/7 and 20/8-3/9: 25% discount on your stay (minimum 7 nights).

## You might like to know
No licence needed for fishing on site. Lake of 113 ha. at 2 km. – cost for a licence per day: € 8. Sea fishing at 12 km. Day sea fishing excursions from St Gilles Croix-de-Vie.

☑ Coarse fishing
☐ Fly fishing
☑ Sea fishing
☑ Lake on site
☐ River on site
☑ Lake nearby (max 5 km)
☐ River nearby (max 5 km)
☐ Licence / permit required
☐ Equipment hire available
☐ Bait and fishing supplies

**Facilities:** Two large, modern sanitary blocks built in traditional style have excellent toilets, showers and washbasins in cubicles. Good facilities for disabled visitors. Attractively tiled areas for babies and children. Two smaller blocks provide additional facilities. Laundry room ('buanderie') with washing machines and dryers. Small shop. Bar counter with terrace. Attractive French restaurant. All facilities available all season. Play area. Bicycle hire. Fishing. WiFi (charged) around bar area. Internet point. Max. 1 dog. Mobile homes, chalets and 'chambres d'hôte' for rent. Off site: Golf and riding 3 km. Beach, sailing, boat launching 12 km. Shops, bars and restaurants in Coëx 2 km. and Saint Gilles Croix-de-Vie 12 km.

**Open:** 9 April - 1 October.

**Directions:** Coëx is 29 km. west of La Roche-sur-Yon via the D938 to Aizenay, then the D6 St Gilles Croix-de-Vie road. Site is south of the village just off the D40 to La Chaize-Giraud and is clearly signed.  GPS: 46.677033, -1.76885

**Charges guide**

| Per unit incl. 2 persons and electricity | € 18,25 - € 39,50 |
| --- | --- |
| incl. 6 persons | € 23,25 - € 52,00 |

# Camping Domaine de la Forêt

Route de Martinet, F-85150 Saint Julien-des-Landes (Vendée)
t: 02 51 46 62 11    e: camping@domainelaforet.com
alanrogers.com/FR85820    www.domainelaforet.com

Accommodation: ☑Pitch ☑Mobile home/chalet ☐Hotel/B&B ☐Apartment

Set in the tranquil and beautiful parkland surrounding an 18th-century château, this lovely site has 200 large pitches, of which 167 are for touring units. There are five units for rent and 28 pitches occupied by tour operators. All are on grass and fully serviced including 6A electricity, some are in shady woodland and others, for sun-worshippers, are more open. The camping area is only a small part of the 50 hectare estate, with a mix of woodland, open meadows and fishing lakes, all accessible to campers. The many outbuildings around the courtyard have been tastefully converted and include a bar and restaurant in the old stables. There are two outdoor swimming pools, one on each side of the château. Children will have a great time here, exploring the vast, unrestricted area and sometimes hidden corners of this site in 'Swallows and Amazons' style. However, parents should note there are open, unfenced fishing lakes and barns with tractors and machinery. The attractive small village with shops and services is within walking distance. The beaches of the Côte de Lumière are just 12 km. away.

## You might like to know
There are three fishing lakes on the campsite and also the nearby Lac de Jaunay. The local Marais also offers numerous angling opportunities.

☑ Coarse fishing
☐ Fly fishing
☐ Sea fishing
☑ Lake on site
☐ River on site
☐ Lake nearby (max 5 km)
☐ River nearby (max 5 km)
☐ Licence / permit required
☐ Equipment hire available
☐ Bait and fishing supplies

**Facilities:** Two large, good quality sanitary blocks include washbasins in cubicles, with good provision for babies and disabled campers. Laundry facilities with washing machines and dryers. Bar/restaurant with TV. Two heated outdoor swimming pools (one for children with slide, one for serious swimmers). Regular evening entertainment, children's clubs and disco (July/Aug). Adventure playground. Tennis. Boules. Fishing lakes. 6-hole swing-golf course (pitch and putt with soft balls) and minigolf. Canoeing trips. WiFi. Only gas barbecues permitted. No double axle caravans accepted. Off site: Equestrian centre, bicycle hire 200 m. Golf and beaches 12 km. ATM La Mothe-Achard 5 km.

**Open:** 15 May - 15 September.

**Directions:** St Julien-des-Landes is 25 km. west of La Roche-sur-Yon, northwest of La Mothe-Achard. From La Mothe-Achard take D12 to St Julien, turn northeast on D55 at crossroads towards Martinet. Site is on left almost immediately (signed). GPS: 46.6432, -1.71198

### Charges guide

| | |
|---|---|
| Per unit incl. 2 persons | € 14,50 - € 29,00 |
| extra person | € 3,00 - € 6,00 |
| child (under 10 yrs) | € 3,00 - € 4,50 |
| electricity (6A) | € 3,00 - € 4,00 |

# Castel Domaine des Forges

Rue des Forges, F-85440 Avrillé (Vendée)
t: 02 51 22 38 85   e: contact@campingdomainedesforges.com
alanrogers.com/FR85930   www.campingdomainedesforges.com

**Accommodation:** ☑Pitch  ☑Mobile home/chalet  ☐Hotel/B&B  ☐Apartment

Le Domaine des Forges has recently been acquired by Cathy and Thierry Pacteau. They already have experience in owning a caravan site, and it is their intention to create a prestige site with the highest quality of services. Arranged in the beautiful grounds of a 16th century manor house, the pitches are generous in size (170-300 m²) and fully serviced including 32A electricity, internet access and cable TV. At present 140 pitches are ready with a further 155 to be developed over the next few years. The owners' aim is to eventually develop a residential site and there are already mobile homes and chalets on site for viewing. Plans for the future include an indoor pool, gym, bar and games room. An area of hardstanding pitches for motorcaravans is also planned.

## You might like to know

Wide choice of splendid sandy beaches including nearby Longeville-sur-Mer and Les Sables d'Olonne. Take a boat trip to l'Ile d'Yeu or explore the green marshes of the Marais.

☑ Coarse fishing
☐ Fly fishing
☐ Sea fishing
☑ Lake on site
☐ River on site
☐ Lake nearby (max 5 km)
☐ River nearby (max 5 km)
☐ Licence / permit required
☐ Equipment hire available
☐ Bait and fishing supplies

**Facilities:** Two toilet blocks with facilities for disabled visitors and babies. Laundry facilities. Takeaway (1/7-31/8). Outdoor pool (heated 1/7-31/8). Tennis. Minigolf. Fishing lake. Off site: Village 400 m. Les Sables d'Olonne 25 km. Vendée beaches 8 km.

**Open:** All year.

**Directions:** Travel south from La Roche-sur-Yon on the D747 for about 21 km. At the D19, turn right for Avrille (about 6 km). At junction with the D949 turn right and first right again into rue des Forges. Site at the end of the road.
GPS: 46.47609, -1.49454

### Charges guide

| Per unit incl. 2 persons, electricity, water and drain | € 16,00 - € 26,00 |
|---|---|
| extra person | € 2,00 - € 6,00 |
| child (2-6 yrs) | free - € 4,00 |
| animal | € 3,00 |

# Monkey Tree Holiday Park

Rejerrah, Newquay TR8 5QR (Cornwall)
t: 01872 572032  e: enquiries@monkeytreeholidaypark.co.uk
alanrogers.com/UK0165  www.monkeytreeholidaypark.co.uk

**Accommodation:** ☑Pitch  ☑Mobile home/chalet  ☐Hotel/B&B  ☐Apartment

Monkey Tree covers 56 acres and boasts an impressive entrance and smart reception. There are 500 pitches with 450 for touring units and 50 caravan holiday homes to rent in their own area. The pitches in the original part of the park benefit from mature hedging which offers a degree of privacy which the newer ones lack, but all have been planted with individual hedges. The pitches are of a good size and most have electricity (13/16A). Serviced pitches with hardstanding are being developed including some extra large pitches which include the use of private facilities in the toilet block. During the holiday season there is much going on at Monkey Tree; all the family should find something to keep them happy. For the little ones there is a morning Kids' Club, for older children there are adventure playgrounds, trampolines, bouncy castles and an amusement arcade. For everyone there is an outdoor heated pool, paddling pool and a sauna. Venturing off the park there are wonderful beaches, a range of watersports to enjoy and places such as the Eden Project and Flambards a must to visit.

## You might like to know

The lake and pond are stocked with carp up to 20lb, tench, roach and bream, with the lake holding the bigger fish. The pond is set in mature surroundings and is an ideal place for either the novice or the experienced angler.

- ☑ Coarse fishing
- ☐ Fly fishing
- ☐ Sea fishing
- ☑ Lake on site
- ☐ River on site
- ☐ Lake nearby (max 5 km)
- ☐ River nearby (max 5 km)
- ☐ Licence / permit required
- ☑ Equipment hire available
- ☑ Bait and fishing supplies

**Facilities:** The original block (refurbished) supplements two new modern timber blocks with heating, providing for all needs including facilities for babies and disabled visitors. Private en-suite facilities for use with the super pitches. Laundry. Motorcaravan services. Gas supplies. Shop (mornings only in low season). Club with entertainment, bar and restaurant (main season and B.Hs). Takeaway (high season). Outdoor pool (Whitsun-end Sept). Trampolines (supervised, with charge). Bouncy castles. Three adventure play areas. Fishing lakes. Off site: Golf, riding, boat launching and sailing 5 miles.

**Open:** All year.

**Directions:** Follow the A30 ignoring all signs for Newquay. At Carland Cross with windmills on the right, carry straight over following signs for Perranporth. After 1 mile turn right at Boxheater Junction on B3285 signed Perranporth and Goonhavern. Follow for 0.5 miles then turn right into Scotland Road for 1 mile to park on the left. GPS: 50.352218, -5.091659

### Charges guide

| Per person | £ 3,75 - £ 6,20 |
| --- | --- |
| child (3-14 yrs) | free - £ 3,75 |
| pitch incl. electricity | £ 3,50 |
| incl. services | £ 7,50 - £ 10,50 |

# South Penquite Farm

South Penquite, Blisland, Bodmin PL30 4LH (Cornwall)
t: 01208 850491   e: thefarm@bodminmoor.co.uk
alanrogers.com/UK0302   www.southpenquite.co.uk

Accommodation: ☑Pitch ☑Mobile home/chalet ☐ Hotel/B&B ☐ Apartment

South Penquite offers real camping with no frills, set on a 200 hectare hill farm high on Bodmin Moor between the villages of Blisland and St Breward. The farm achieved organic status in 2001 and runs a flock of 300 ewes and a herd of 40 cattle and horses. The camping is small scale and intended to have a low impact on the surrounding environment. Tents or simple motorcaravans (no caravans) can pitch around the edge of three walled fields, roughly cut in the midst of the moor. You can find shelter or a view. Four Yurts (round Mongolian tents) are available to rent in one field, complete with wood burning stoves – quite original. Camp fires are permitted with wood available from the farmhouse. You will also find horses, ponies, chickens, geese, ducks and turkeys which show their approval or not by the skin around their necks changing colour! A farm walk of some two miles takes you over most of the farm and some of the moor taking in a Bronze Age hut settlement, the river and a standing stone. It is also possible to fish for brown trout on the farm's stretch of the De Lank river – a tributary of the Camel.

## You might like to know

Under the West Country Rivers Trust West Country Angling Passport scheme you can now fish for brown trout on the site's beautiful 1400 metre stretch of the De Lank river – a tributary of the Camel.

☑ Coarse fishing
☐ Fly fishing
☐ Sea fishing
☐ Lake on site
☑ River on site
☐ Lake nearby (max 5 km)
☐ River nearby (max 5 km)
☑ Licence / permit required
☐ Equipment hire available
☐ Bait and fishing supplies

**Facilities:** A smart new pine clad toilet block, with a separate provision of four family-sized showers, with solar heated rainwater. Two covered dishwashing sinks (H&C) and two outside Belfast sinks. Washing machine and dryer. Small fridge and freezer. Home produced lamb, burgers and sausages. LPG gas. Facilities for field studies. Bushcraft days. Fishing (requires an EA rod licence and tokens available from the West Country Rivers Trust). Dogs are not accepted. Off site: Walking. Riding and cycling 1 mile. Inns 1.5 and 2.5 miles.

**Open:** 1 May - 1 November.

**Directions:** On the A30 over Bodmin Moor pass Jamaica Inn and sign for Colliford Lake and watch for St Breward sign (to right) immediately at end of dual-carriageway. Follow this narrow road for 2 miles ignoring any turns to left or right. Also ignore right turn to St Breward just before the South Penquite sign. Follow track over stone bridge beside ford through farm gate and then bear to left to camping fields. Walk back to book in at Farm House. GPS: 50.5445, -4.671833

### Charges guide

| | |
|---|---|
| Per person | £ 6,00 |
| child (5-16 yrs) | £ 3,00 |

No credit cards.

# Cofton Country Holidays

Starcross, EX6 8RP Dawlish (Devon)
t: **01626 890111**  e: **info@coftonholidays.co.uk**
alanrogers.com/UK0970  www.coftonholidays.co.uk

Accommodation: ☑Pitch  ☑Mobile home/chalet  ☐Hotel/B&B  ☐Apartment

A popular and well run family park, Cofton is 1.5 miles from a sandy beach at Dawlish Warren. It has space for 450 touring units on a variety of fields and meadows with beautiful country views. Although not individually marked, there is never a feeling of overcrowding. The smaller, more mature fields, including a pleasant old orchard for tents only, are well terraced. There are some 450 electrical connections (10A), 16 hardstandings and 14 'super' pitches. One area has 66 park-owned holiday homes for let or to buy. A well designed, central complex overlooking the pool and decorated with flowers and hanging baskets, houses reception, a shop and off-licence and a bar lounge, the 'Cofton Swan', where bar meals are available. The adjacent supervised, kidney-shaped, heated pool with paddling pool, has lots of grassy space for sunbathing. Coarse fishing is available in five lakes on the park. The adjoining unspoilt woodland of 50 acres provides wonderful views across the Exe estuary and a woodland trail of two miles to Dawlish Warren.

## Special offers

Free fishing between November and Mid March. Short breaks available out of season. Save 25% touring/camping in low - high season when you book 5 or more nights in advance.

## You might like to know

Fishing tackle shop on site with tackle hire available. On site there is also a bar serving meals, takeaway, outdoor heated swimming pool and shop (check website for opening times).

☑ **Coarse fishing**
☐ **Fly fishing**
☐ **Sea fishing**
☑ **Lake on site**
☐ **River on site**
☐ **Lake nearby (max 5 km)**
☐ **River nearby (max 5 km)**
☑ **Licence / permit required**
☑ **Equipment hire available**
☑ **Bait and fishing supplies**

**Facilities:** Toilet facilities comprise six blocks, well placed for all areas, one of a very high standard. Facilities for disabled visitors and babies. Hair dryers. Two launderettes. Gas available. Ice pack hire service. Bar lounge serving bar snacks. TV. Shop (1/4-28/10). Fish and chip shop also serving breakfast (1/4-30/10). Swimming pool (overall length 100 ft. open Spr.B.H-mid Sept). Games room. Adventure playground in the woods overlooking the pools and two other well equipped play areas. Coarse fishing (from £ 25 per rod for 7 days, discount for senior citizens outside July/Aug). Off site: Beach and boat launching 1.5 miles. Woodland walks/pub 0.5 miles. Golf 3 miles. Riding 5 miles. Bicycle hire in Dawlish.

**Open:** All year.

**Directions:** Access to the park is off the A379 road 3 miles north of Dawlish, just after Cockwood harbour village.
GPS: 50.6126, -3.460467

**Charges guide**

| Per unit incl. 2 persons | |
|---|---|
| and electricity | £ 13,00 - £ 27,50 |
| hardstanding pitch | £ 16,50 - £ 29,50 |
| serviced pitch | £ 19,50 - £ 33,50 |
| extra person (over 2 yrs) | £ 2,50 - £ 4,75 |

# Beacon Hill Touring Park

Blandford Road North, BH16 6AB Poole (Dorset)
t: **01202 631631**  e: bookings@beaconhilltouringpark.co.uk
alanrogers.com/UK2180  www.beaconhilltouringpark.co.uk

**Accommodation:** ☑Pitch ☑Mobile home/chalet ☐Hotel/B&B ☐Apartment

Beacon Hill is located in a marvellous, natural environment of partly wooded heathland, with certain areas of designated habitation for protected species such as sand lizards and the Dartford Warbler, but there is also easy access to main routes. Wildlife ponds encourage dragonflies and other species but fishing is also possible. Conservation is obviously important in such a special area but one can ramble at will over the 30 acres with the hilltop walk a must. Grassy open spaces provide 170 pitches, 151 with 10A electricity, on sandy grass which is sometimes uneven. Of these, 50 are for tents only and a few are seasonal. The undulating nature of the land and the trees allows for discrete areas to be allocated for varying needs, for example young families near the play area, families with teenagers close to the bar/games room, those with dogs near the dog walking area, and young people further away. The park provides a wide range of facilities, including an open air swimming pool and a tennis court. It is well situated for beaches, Poole harbour and ferries for France or the Channel Isles.

## Special offers
Special discounts available.
Please visit website for details:
www.beaconhilltouringpark.co.uk.

## You might like to know
The Park consists of 30 acres of partly wooded heath land hosting an abundance of wildlife and natural beauty. Certain areas are designated Special Areas of Conservation.

☑ Coarse fishing
☐ Fly fishing
☐ Sea fishing
☑ Lake on site
☐ River on site
☐ Lake nearby (max 5 km)
☐ River nearby (max 5 km)
☑ Licence / permit required
☐ Equipment hire available
☐ Bait and fishing supplies

**Facilities:** Two fully equipped toilet blocks include facilities for disabled visitors. Laundry facilities. Well stocked shop at reception. Coffee bar and takeaway (main season). Bar (July/Aug, B.Hs, half-terms). Heated swimming pool (mid May-mid Sept). All weather tennis court (charges). Adventure play areas including a hideaway. Games room with pool tables and amusement machines. TV room. Internet (WiFi). Fishing (charged). Off site: Poole harbour and ferries 3 miles. Riding 2 miles. Bicycle hire 3 miles. Brownsea Island, Studland beach with Sandbanks ferry and the Purbecks near.

**Open:** 17 March - end September.

**Directions:** Park is about 3 miles north of Poole. Take A350 (towards Blandford) at roundabout where A350 joins A35. Park signed to the right (northeast) after about 400 yards.
GPS: 50.74953, -2.03446

### Charges guide

| | |
|---|---|
| Per unit incl. 2 persons and electricity | £ 13,50 - £ 35,00 |
| extra person | £ 3,50 - £ 6,50 |
| child (3-15 yrs) | £ 2,50 - £ 3,00 |
| dog | £ 1,00 - £ 1,50 |

# Chichester Lakeside Park

Vinnetrow Road, Chichester PO20 1QH (West Sussex)
t: **0845 815 9775**   e: **lakeside@ParkHolidays.com**
alanrogers.com/UK2875   www.parkholidaysuk.com

**Accommodation:** ☐ Pitch  ☑ Mobile home/chalet  ☐ Hotel/B&B  ☐ Apartment

Located just outside the historic city of Chichester, this large site is part of the Park Holidays group. Please note that there are no touring pitches on this site. Accommodation is provided in a range of fully equipped mobile homes, available for rent. This is a mecca for anglers with no fewer than 10 large fishing lakes. The site is set in 150 acres of Sussex countryside, but also within easy access of a sandy beach and the traditional resort of Bognor Regis. This is a lively site in peak season with a newly refurbished entertainment centre boasting a choice of bars and dining options. On-site amenities include a swimming pool, and a children's club (5-14 years) is organised in peak season. Chichester is an attractive city, with its 12th century cathedral of particular interest. The city is also home to the Festival Theatre, one of England's flagship cultural centres. Bognor Regis was originally a smuggling village but it became popular as a holiday resort in the 19th century.

**Facilities:** Bar. Restaurant. Entertainment complex. Supermarket. Swimming pool. Fishing. Children's play area. Children's club. Tourist information. Mobile homes for rent (no touring pitches). Off site: Nearby resort of Bognor Regis (good selection of cafés, restaurants and shops). Walking and cycle routes. Chichester (cathedral city).

**Open:** 1 March - 31 October.

**Directions:** From Chichester take the A27 towards Havant and Brighton. At the Bognor Road roundabout take the fourth exit onto Vinnetrow Road (Pagham), to the site. GPS: 50.823885, -0.75119

**Charges guide**

Contact the park for details.

## You might like to know

Lakeside Park offers 150 acres of fishing lakes for all keen fishermen – bring your rod for some peace and quiet while on holiday. NRA licence required.

☐ Coarse fishing
☑ Fly fishing
☐ Sea fishing
☑ Lake on site
☐ River on site
☐ Lake nearby (max 5 km)
☐ River nearby (max 5 km)
☑ Licence / permit required
☐ Equipment hire available
☐ Bait and fishing supplies

# Homestead Lake Park

Thorpe Road, Weeley, Clacton-on-Sea CO16 9JN (Essex)
t: **01255 833492**  e: **lakepark@homesteadcaravans.co.uk**
alanrogers.com/UK3300  www.homesteadlake.co.uk

**Accommodation:** ☑Pitch ☑Mobile home/chalet ☐ Hotel/B&B ☐ Apartment

This well laid out, 25-acre park was opened in 2002. It is hidden from the road at the rear of Homestead Caravans sales area and workshops in the countryside of the Tendring district, at Weeley near Clacton. It offers 50 fully serviced, hardstanding pitches on gently sloping ground overlooking a fishing lake and recently-built holiday lodge accommodation on the other side of the lake. Tents accepted for short stays only on a limited number of pitches. The park makes an ideal spot to stay either for fishing, for a relaxing weekend, or as a base for touring this part of Essex. A special area has been added to allow wheelchair users to fish. You could even arrange for your caravan to be serviced or repairs to be made while you stay. Homestead also has a large accessories superstore and café, where breakfast is recommended as a start to your day.

## You might like to know

Homestead Lake Park has been developed around a central coarse fishing lake stocked with good sized carp, perch, tench and roach.

- ☑ Coarse fishing
- ☐ Fly fishing
- ☐ Sea fishing
- ☑ Lake on site
- ☐ River on site
- ☐ Lake nearby (max 5 km)
- ☐ River nearby (max 5 km)
- ☑ Licence / permit required
- ☐ Equipment hire available
- ☑ Bait and fishing supplies

**Facilities:** The toilet block offers clean and spacious facilities including an en-suite unit for disabled visitors. Baby changing facilities. Coffee shop/café and snack bar. Fishing lake. Woodland walks. Caravan sales, workshops and accessory shop. A large rally field is also available. Off site: The site is ideally situated for visiting the many attractions of this holiday area. The towns of Clacton-on-Sea, Frinton, Harwich and Brightlingsea are all within a 10-mile radius and the heart of 'Constable' country, with Flatford Mill and Dedham, is a short drive away.

**Open:** 1 March - 31 October.

**Directions:** From Colchester take A120, then A133 signed Clacton. At roundabout, turn left on B1033 into Weeley and site and showrooms are on left just past council offices.
GPS: 51.85989, 1.12021

### Charges guide

| Per unit incl. 2 persons and electricity | £ 15,00 - £ 22,00 |
| --- | --- |
| extra person | £ 4,00 |
| child (under 18 yrs) | £ 2,00 |
| dog | £ 2,00 |

# Tallington Lakes Touring Park

Barholm Road, Tallington, Stamford PE9 4RJ (Lincolnshire)
t: **01778 347000**  e: **info@tallington.com**
alanrogers.com/UK3760  www.tallington.com

Accommodation: ☑Pitch  ☑Mobile home/chalet  ☐ Hotel/B&B  ☐ Apartment

This well maintained and attractive 160-acre site surrounds over 200 acres of clean, spring fed water that provides many watersport activities including water-ski, jet-ski, sailing, windsurfing, canoeing, pedaloes and angling; along with a Pro Shop for water sports. In addition there is a 120 m. high, floodlit dry ski slope and a 15 m. tower for climbing and abseiling. Of the 338 pitches, 88 are in a separate area for touring and 46 have 10A electricity. They are level, in groups, separated by some hedging and are either on grass or hard standing. Some mature trees give a little shade. The two well appointed toilet blocks at each end of the site may be a considerable distance from some of the pitches. The bar/restaurant with attractive terrace overlooks the swimming pool and the lake beyond. Lake swimming is not allowed. Stamford, with its famous old coaching inns is only five miles away, and Peterborough with many shops, parks and modern cathedral is only a few miles further. The surrounding area has much to offer.

## You might like to know

Most species of coarse fish can be caught here but please note that Tallington Lakes is primarily a watersports centre, and as a result all floating craft have priority.

☑ **Coarse fishing**
☐ Fly fishing
☐ Sea fishing
☑ **Lake on site**
☐ River on site
☐ Lake nearby (max 5 km)
☐ River nearby (max 5 km)
☑ **Licence / permit required**
☐ Equipment hire available
☐ Bait and fishing supplies

**Facilities:** The heated sanitary unit has facilities for babies, small children and campers with disabilities. Additional WCs and showers (also used by the water skiers). Laundry and dishwashing facilities. Motorcaravan service point. Bar and restaurant. Swimming and paddling pools (charged). Climbing wall. Go-karting. Watersports. Fishing. Dry-ski slope, snowboard centre and tennis. Small, well fenced, adventure style playground. Off site: Bus stop 1 mile. Golf, riding and bicycle hire 5 miles. Stamford 5 miles, Peterborough, 11 miles.

**Open:** All year.

**Directions:** From A16, midway between Stamford and Market Deeping, just east of the railway crossing at Tallington, turn north into Barholm Road. Site entrance is on the right in 0.3 miles (site is signed). GPS: 52.67007, -0.37940

**Charges guide**

| Per unit incl. 2 persons and electricity | £ 20,00 - £ 30,00 |
| --- | --- |
| extra person | £ 5,00 |
| dog (max. 2 per unit) | £ 5,00 |

# Smeaton's Lakes Touring Park

Great North Road, South Muskham, Newark-on-Trent NG23 6ED (Nottinghamshire)
t: **01636 605088**  e: **lesley@smeatonslakes.co.uk**
alanrogers.com/UK3940  www.smeatonslakes.co.uk

Accommodation: ☑Pitch  ☑Mobile home/chalet  ☐Hotel/B&B  ☐Apartment

This 82 acre site is really ideal for anglers, with four fishing lakes (coarse, carp and pike) and river fishing on the Trent. There are 130 pitches of which 100 have electricity connections (16A). Non-anglers might choose this park if visiting antique fairs or events at nearby Newark Showground, or Newark town (1 mile) with its castle, air museum and various weekly markets. During your stay, you might visit Southwell Cathedral, Sherwood Forest, Clumber Park, Lincoln with its castle and cathedral or Nottingham with its Lace Hall, Castle and Caves.

## You might like to know

With several ponds, carp and coarse lakes, and a good stretch of the River Trent, there is something here for every coarse fisherman.

- ☑ Coarse fishing
- ☐ Fly fishing
- ☐ Sea fishing
- ☑ Lake on site
- ☐ River on site
- ☐ Lake nearby (max 5 km)
- ☐ River nearby (max 5 km)
- ☑ Licence / permit required
- ☐ Equipment hire available
- ☑ Bait and fishing supplies

**Facilities:** Two toilet blocks (with keypad access) are heated and include a good unit for disabled visitors, but no laundry room. Laundry and dishwashing sinks are outside. Reception keeps gas, soft drinks, dairy produce, etc. and newspapers can be ordered. On-site concessions for lake and river fishing. Entry barrier with key access. Security cameras and night-time height barrier (about 6 ft). Off site: Bus stop at the end of the entry lane – buses run into Newark every hour until 10 pm. Riding and boat launching 2 miles. Golf 3 miles.

**Open:** All year.

**Directions:** Park is a mile north of Newark on the old Great North Road. From south on the A1, take A46 west (signed Newark, Leicester) and turn north on A6065/A616 towards South Muskham. From southwest (M1/A46) turn north off Newark bypass on A6065/A616 as above. From north on A1 leave B6325 (Newark) continue south through South Muskham. Follow signs for Newark. GPS: 53.0936, -0.820667

### Charges guide

| | |
|---|---|
| Per unit incl. 2 persons | £ 12,00 - £ 13,00 |
| with electricity (16A) | £ 15,00 - £ 18,00 |
| extra person | £ 3,00 |
| child | £ 1,50 |

# Croft Farm Water & Leisure Park

Bredon's Hardwick, Tewkesbury GL20 7EE (Gloucestershire)
t: 01684 772321   e: enquiries@croftfarmleisure.co.uk
alanrogers.com/UK4150   www.croftfarmleisure.co.uk

Accommodation: ☑Pitch ☑Mobile home/chalet ☐Hotel/B&B ☐Apartment

Croft Farm is an AALA licensed Watersports Centre with Royal Yachting Association approved tuition available for windsurfing, sailing, kayaking and canoeing. The lakeside campsite has around 96 level pitches, with electric hook-ups (10A), but there are many seasonal units, leaving around 36 pitches for tourers, plus some tent pitches. There are 36 gravel hardstandings with very little shade or shelter. 'Gym and Tonic' is a fully equipped gymnasium with qualified instructors, sunbed and sauna. Sports massage, aromatherapy and beauty treatments are available by appointment. Activity holidays for families and groups are organised. Campers can use their own non-powered boats on the lake with reduced launching fees and there is river fishing. There are plans to include a launch ramp onto the river. Climb Bredon Hill (2 miles) for a panoramic view of the Severn and Avon Valleys. Places of interest include Bredon Barn, pottery and church, and the historic town of Tewkesbury with its Abbey, theatre and indoor swimming pool.

## You might like to know

Croft Farm is situated in the River Avon Valley adjacent to a lake. A footpath meanders through the meadow to the River Avon and free fishing is available to all campers.

☑ Coarse fishing
☐ Fly fishing
☐ Sea fishing
☑ Lake on site
☐ River on site
☐ Lake nearby (max 5 km)
☑ River nearby (max 5 km)
☐ Licence / permit required
☐ Equipment hire available
☐ Bait and fishing supplies

**Facilities:** A recently modernised building has excellent facilities with spacious hot showers, plus some dishwashing sinks. A heated unit in the main building is always open and best for cooler months; this provides further WCs, washbasins and showers, laundry and facilities for disabled visitors. Gas. Cafe/bar (Fri-Sun low season, daily at other times). Takeaway. Gym. Playground. River fishing. Barrier and toilet block key (£5 deposit). WiFi in the clubhouse. Off site: Pub opposite. Tewkesbury 1.5 miles. Golf 3 miles. Riding 8 miles.

**Open:** 1 March - 31 December.

**Directions:** Bredon's Hardwick is midway between Tewkesbury and Bredon on the B4080. Site entrance opposite 'Cross Keys Inn'. From M5 exit 9 take A438 (Tewkesbury), at first lights turn right into Shannon Way. Turn right at next lights, into Northway Lane, cross motorway bridge. Turn left into housing estate and cross second bridge. At T-junction turn right on B4080, site is on left. GPS: 52.015967, -2.130267

### Charges guide

| | |
|---|---|
| Per unit incl. 2 persons, electricity and awning | £ 16,00 |
| extra person (over 3 yrs) | £ 3,50 |
| dog | £ 1,00 |

# Fforest Fields Caravan Park

Hundred House, Builth Wells LD1 5RT (Powys)
t: **01982 570406**  e: **office@fforestfields.co.uk**
alanrogers.com/UK6320  www.fforestfields.co.uk

**Accommodation:** ☑Pitch ☑Mobile home/chalet ☐Hotel/B&B ☐Apartment

This secluded 'different' park is set on a family hill farm in the heart of Radnorshire. Truly rural, there are glorious views and a distinctly family atmosphere. This is simple country camping and caravanning at its best, without man-made distractions or intrusions. The facilities include 80 large pitches on level grass on a spacious and peaceful, carefully landscaped field by a stream. Electrical connections (mostly 16A) are available and there are 17 hardstanding pitches, also with electricity. Several additional areas without electricity are provided for tents. There are two new lakes, one for boating and fly fishing, the other for coarse fishing. A new reception and toilet block are planned. George and Kate, the enthusiastic owners, have opened up much of the farm for moderate or ample woodland and moorland trails which can be enjoyed with much wildlife to see. Indeed wildlife is actively encouraged with nesting boxes for owls, songbirds and bats, by leaving field margins wild to encourage small mammals and by yearly tree planting.

## You might like to know

Off site, why not try the Upper Wye Passport, a roving voucher system allowing you to fish for wild trout, salmon and winter grayling in the delightful head waters and tributaries of the Wye.

- ☑ Coarse fishing
- ☐ Fly fishing
- ☐ Sea fishing
- ☑ Lake on site
- ☐ River on site
- ☐ Lake nearby (max 5 km)
- ☐ River nearby (max 5 km)
- ☐ Licence / permit required
- ☐ Equipment hire available
- ☑ Bait and fishing supplies

**Facilities:** The toilet facilities are acceptable with a baby bath. Dishwashing and laundry facilities including washing machines and dryer. Milk, eggs, orange juice and gas are sold in reception, otherwise there are few other on-site facilities. Fishing. Torches are useful. Off site: The village of Hundred House (1 mile) has a pub. Bicycle hire and golf 5 miles. Riding 10 miles.

**Open:** Easter - 17 November.

**Directions:** Park is 4 miles east of Builth Wells near the village of Hundred House on A481. Follow brown signs. GPS: 52.17121, -3.31621

**Charges guide**

| | |
|---|---|
| Per person | £ 3,50 |
| child | £ 2,50 |
| pitch | £ 4,50 |
| electricity | £ 2,50 |
| dog | free |

Special low season rates for senior citizens. No credit cards.

# Hoddom Castle Caravan Park

Hoddom, Lockerbie DG11 1AS (Dumfries and Galloway)
t: **01576 300251**   e: **hoddomcastle@aol.com**
alanrogers.com/UK6910  www.hoddomcastle.co.uk

**Accommodation:** ☑Pitch  ☑Mobile home/chalet  ☐ Hotel/B&B  ☐ Apartment

The park around Hoddom Castle is landscaped, spacious and well laid out on mainly sloping ground with many mature and beautiful trees, originally part of an arboretum. The drive to the site is just under a mile long with a one way system. Many of the 120 numbered pitches have good views of the castle and have gravel hardstanding with grass for awnings. Most have electrical connections (16A). In front of the castle are flat fields used for tents and caravans with a limited number of electricity hook-ups. The oldest part of Hoddom Castle itself is a 16th century Borders Pele Tower, or fortified Keep. The site's bar and restaurant have been developed in the courtyard area from the coach houses, and the main ladies' toilet block was the stables. Amenities include a comfortable bar lounge with a TV. The park's 9-hole golf course is in an attractive setting alongside the Annan river, where fishing is possible for salmon and trout (tickets available). Coarse fishing is also possible elsewhere on the estate. This is a peaceful base from which to explore historic southwest Scotland.

## You might like to know

Hoddom and Kinmount Estates owns 2.5 miles of the River Annan which is mainly a salmon and sea trout river. The sea trout start to run in May with the main run in June and July.

☐ Coarse fishing
☑ Fly fishing
☐ Sea fishing
☐ Lake on site
☑ River on site
☐ Lake nearby (max 5 km)
☐ River nearby (max 5 km)
☑ Licence / permit required
☐ Equipment hire available
☐ Bait and fishing supplies

**Facilities:** The main toilet block can be heated and is very well appointed. Washbasins in cubicles, 3 en-suite cubicles with WC and basin (one with baby facilities) and an en-suite shower unit for disabled visitors. Two further tiled blocks, kept very clean, provide washbasins and WCs only. Well equipped laundry room at the castle. Motorcaravan service point. Licensed shop at reception (gas available). Bar, restaurant and takeaway (restricted opening outside high season). Games room. Large, grass play area. Crazy golf. Mountain bike trail. Fishing. Golf. Guided walks (high season). Caravan storage. Off site: Tennis nearby.

**Open:** 1 April - 30 October.

**Directions:** Leave A74M at exit 19 (Ecclefechan) and follow signs to park. Leave A75 at Annan junction (west end of Annan by-pass) and follow signs. GPS: 55.041367, -3.311

### Charges guide

| Per unit incl. 2 persons | £ 9,00 - £ 16,00 |
| --- | --- |
| incl. electricity | £ 12,00 - £ 19,00 |
| extra person | £ 3,00 |
| child (7-16 yrs) | £ 1,00 |

# Glendaruel Caravan Park

Glendaruel PA22 3AB (Argyll and Bute)
t: 01369 820267  e: mail@glendaruelcaravanpark.co.uk
alanrogers.com/UK7860  www.glendaruelcaravanpark.co.uk

**Accommodation:** ☑Pitch  ☑Mobile home/chalet  ☐ Hotel/B&B  ☐ Apartment

Glendaruel is in South Argyll, in the area of Scotland bounded by the Kyles of Bute and Loch Fyne, yet is less than two hours by road from Glasgow and serviced by ferries from Gourock and the Isle of Bute. There is also a service between Tarbert and Portavadie. Set in the peaceful wooded gardens of the former Glendaruel House in a secluded glen surrounded by the Cowal hills, it makes an ideal centre for touring this beautiful area. The park takes 35 units on numbered hardstandings with electricity (10A), plus 15 tents, on flat oval meadows bordered by over 50 varieties of mature trees. In a separate area are 28 privately owned holiday homes and 2 for rent. The converted stables of the original house provide an attractive little shop selling basics, local produce, venison, salmon, wines (some Scottish!) and tourist gifts. Glendaruel is a park for families with young children or for older couples to relax and to enjoy the beautiful views across the Sound of Bute from Tighnabruaich or the botanical gardens which flourish in the climate. The Craig family provides a warm welcome and will advise you where to eat and what to do – they are justifiably proud of their park and its beautiful environment.

## You might like to know

Fly fishing for salmon and sea trout on the River Ruel. Permits are available for sale in the site shop for the Ruel.

☐ Coarse fishing
☑ Fly fishing
☐ Sea fishing
☐ Lake on site
☑ River on site
☐ Lake nearby (max 5 km)
☐ River nearby (max 5 km)
☑ Licence / permit required
☐ Equipment hire available
☐ Bait and fishing supplies

**Facilities:** The toilet block is ageing but it is kept very neat and tidy and can be heated. Washing machine and dryer. A covered area has picnic tables for use in bad weather and dishwashing sinks. Shop (hours may be limited in low season). Gas available. Games room. Behind the laundry is a children's play centre for under 12s and additional play field. Fishing. Torches advised. Off site: Sea fishing and boat slipway 5 miles, adventure centre (assault courses, abseiling and rafting) and sailing school close. Golf 12 miles.

**Open:** 28 March - 26 October.

**Directions:** Entrance is off A886 road 13 miles south of Strachur. Alternatively there are two ferry services from Gourock to Dunoon, then on B836 which joins the A886 about 4 miles south of the park - this route not recommended for touring caravans. Do not use sat nav as this takes you along a very narrow back road and there is no entrance from here. Note: the park has discount arrangements with Western Ferries so contact the park before making arrangements.
GPS: 56.033967, -5.212833

## Charges guide

| | |
|---|---|
| Per person | £ 3,00 |
| child (3-15 yrs) | £ 1,50 |
| pitch incl. electricity | £ 10,00 |

# Lough Ree (East) Caravan Park

Ballykeeran, Athlone (Co. Westmeath)
t: 090 647 8561  e: athlonecamping@eircom.net
alanrogers.com/IR8960

Accommodation: ☑Pitch ☑Mobile home/chalet ☐Hotel/B&B ☐Apartment

This touring park is alongside the river, screened by trees but reaching the water's edge. Drive into the small village of Ballykeeran and the park is discreetly located behind the main street. The top half of the site is in a woodland situation and after the reception and sanitary block, Lough Ree comes into view and the remaining pitches run down to the shoreline. There are 60 pitches, 20 with hardstanding and 52 with 6A electricity. A wooden chalet houses a pool room with an open fire and a campers' kitchen (although there are no cooking facilities). With fishing right on the doorstep there are boats for hire locally and the site has its own private mooring buoys, plus a dinghy slip and harbour. A restaurant and 'singing' pub are close.

## You might like to know
This site has its own jetty and boat slip. Ideal for angling, boating, windsurfing, sailing and also canoeing.

☑ Coarse fishing
☐ Fly fishing
☐ Sea fishing
☑ Lake on site
☐ River on site
☐ Lake nearby (max 5 km)
☐ River nearby (max 5 km)
☑ Licence / permit required
☑ Equipment hire available
☐ Bait and fishing supplies

**Facilities:** The toilet block is clean without being luxurious. Hot showers (€ 1). Dishwashing sinks outside. Laundry room (wash and dry € 8). Wooden chalet housing pool room and campers' kitchen (no cooking facilities). Off site: Riding 4 km. Golf 8 km.

**Open:** 1 April - 30 September.

**Directions:** From Athlone take the N55 towards Longford for 4.8 km. Park is in the village of Ballykeeran, clearly signed. GPS: 53.44815, -7.88992

**Charges guide**

Per unit incl. 2 persons and electricity   € 23,00

No credit cards.

# Blackwater Valley Caravan Park

Mallow-Killarney Road, Fermoy (Co. Cork)
t: 025 321 47
alanrogers.com/IR9470

**Accommodation:** ☑Pitch ☑Mobile home/chalet ☐ Hotel/B&B ☐ Apartment

The location of this park provides the best of both worlds, as it backs onto green fields adjacent to the Blackwater river, yet is within 200 metres of Fermoy town. Pat and Nora Ryan live overlooking the park which ensures supervision and prompt attention. Well situated for touring, there are 25 pitches, all with hardstanding and electricity connections (13A). Water taps are convenient to all pitches. Considerable additional space for tents is available towards the rear of the park. There are five caravan holiday homes to rent. Fermoy provides local amenities, such as a cinema, restaurants and pubs, many of these providing traditional music. The town park has a leisure centre with pool, and an excellent play area is 100 metres on foot. The park owners also own the stretch of the Blackwater river that runs alongside – a huge plus for all campers who fancy trying their hand at fishing. A site suitable for motorcaravanners due to the proximinity to the town centre. Many other attractions are within easy reach of the park.

## You might like to know
The Blackwater river is one of Fermoy's major attractions and is very popular for its salmon and coarse fishing.

☑ Coarse fishing
☐ Fly fishing
☐ Sea fishing
☐ Lake on site
☐ River on site
☐ Lake nearby (max 5 km)
☑ River nearby (max 5 km)
☑ Licence / permit required
☐ Equipment hire available
☐ Bait and fishing supplies

**Facilities:** Modern, tiled toilet block provides the usual facilities including an en-suite shower room for disabled visitors. Laundry room with ironing facilities. Campers' kitchen with cooking facilities and dining area. TV and games room. Motorcaravan service point. Off site: Fishing adjacent to park. Internet access 100 m. Bicycle hire 1 km. Golf 3.5 km. Beach 35 km. Petrol station with gas across the road.

**Open:** 15 March - 31 October.

**Directions:** In Fermoy town take the N72 for Mallow. Park is 200 m. from the junction. GPS: 52.141498, -8.281873

### Charges guide

| | |
|---|---|
| Per unit incl. 2 persons | € 17,00 |
| extra person | € 5,00 |
| child | € 2,00 |
| electricity | € 3,50 |

No credit cards.

# Fleming's White Bridge

Ballycasheen Road, Killarney (Co. Kerry)
t: **064 663 1590**  e: **info@killarneycamping.com**
alanrogers.com/IR9620  www.killarneycamping.com

**Accommodation:** ☑Pitch ☑Mobile home/chalet ☐ Hotel/B&B ☐ Apartment

The main road from Cork to Killarney (N22) runs through the gentle valley of the Flesk river. Between the two sits Fleming's White Bridge Camping Park. Its ten hectare site is within comfortable walking distance of Killarney centre. Surrounded by mature broad leafed trees, the park is flat, landscaped and generously adorned with flowers and shrubs. It comprises 92 pitches, the majority for touring caravans on well kept grass pitches with electricity hook-ups, although some have concrete handstanding and some pitches are reserved for tents. Well distributed around the park are three well appointed toilet blocks. This is obviously a site of which the owners are very proud. Hillary and Moira Fleming personally supervise the reception and grounds, maintaining high standards of hygiene, cleanliness and tidiness. In high season they even find time to organise on-site activities that keep children happy and parents relaxed. The park's location so close to Ireland's premier tourism centre makes this park an ideal base to explore Killarney and the southwest.

## You might like to know

Fleming's White Bridge quietly nestles on the banks of the river Flesk in a well landscaped rural setting, one mile east of Killarney.

☑ **Coarse fishing**
☐ Fly fishing
☐ Sea fishing
☐ Lake on site
☑ **River on site**
☐ Lake nearby (max 5 km)
☐ River nearby (max 5 km)
☑ **Licence / permit required**
☐ Equipment hire available
☐ Bait and fishing supplies

**Facilities:** Three high-standard toilet blocks. Motorcaravan service point. Campers' drying room and two laundries. Small shop (1/6-1/9). Two TV rooms and a games room. Fishing (advice and permits provided). Canoeing (own canoes). Bicycle hire. Woodland walks. Off site: Riding 3 km. Golf 2 km.

**Open:** 15 March - 31 October.

**Directions:** From Cork and Mallow: at the N72/N22 junction continue towards Killarney and take first turn left (signed Ballycasheen Road). Proceed for 300 m. to archway entrance on left. From Limerick: follow N22 Cork road. Pass Super Valu and The Heights Hotel, take first right (signed Ballycasheen Road) and continue as above. From Kenmare: On N71, pass Gleneagles Hotel and Flesk Bridge. Turn right at traffic lights into Woodlawn Road and Ballycasheen Road and continue 2 km. to archway.
GPS: 52.05595, -9.47458

**Charges guide**

| Per unit incl. 2 persons and electricity | € 30,00 - € 31,00 |
| --- | --- |
| extra person | € 8,00 |
| child | € 3,00 - € 11,00 |

No credit cards.

# Donoghues White Villa Farm

Killarney - Cork Road N22, Lissivigeen, Killarney (Co. Kerry)
t: **064 662 0671**  e: **killarneycamping@eircom.net**
alanrogers.com/IR9630  www.killarneycaravanpark.com

**Accommodation:** ☑ Pitch  ☑ Mobile home/chalet  ☐ Hotel/B&B  ☐ Apartment

This is a very pleasing small touring park in scenic surroundings off the N22 Cork-Killarney road. Set in the countryside, surrounded by green fields, yet is only five minutes away from Killarney town. There are many trees and shrubs around the park but dominant is a magnificent view of the MacGillicuddy's Reeks. There are 30 pitches for caravans and tents, 20 with hardstanding and a grass area for awnings, electricity (10A), water points and night lighting. One pitch is designated for disabled campers and there is a key-operated en suite facility for their use. An unusual novelty is that old school desks are placed in pairs around the site as picnic tables, plus an antique green telephone box. One can also enjoy walking through the oak wood, fishing on the Flesk or visiting the site's own National Farm Museum. There is a pleasant old-fashioned charm about the White Villa park. Some visitors might fondly describe it as 'camping as it used to be', while others might argue that 'camping as it should be' would better suit, since most of White Villa's facilities compare well with any competitor in the area.

## You might like to know

The O'Donoghue family have been welcoming visitors to their peaceful touring park since 1962. The adjacent River Flesk offers some fine fishing.

☑ Coarse fishing
☐ Fly fishing
☐ Sea fishing
☐ Lake on site
☐ River on site
☐ Lake nearby (max 5 km)
☑ River nearby (max 5 km)
☑ Licence / permit required
☐ Equipment hire available
☐ Bait and fishing supplies

**Facilities:** The toilet block, a sandstone coloured building, is kept spotlessly clean and houses showers on payment (€ 1,00), a good toilet/shower room for disabled visitors, laundry room and dishwashing sinks. Motorcaravan service area. Campers' kitchen with TV. Play area. Max. 2 dogs (not certain breeds). Daily coach tours from park. Off site: Riding, golf and bicycle hire 3 km. Pub/restaurant 1 km. Killarney town 5 minutes, the National Park is 10 minutes away.

**Open:** Easter - 2 October.

**Directions:** Park is 3 km. east from Killarney town on N22 Cork road. Park entrance is 300 m. east of N22/N72 roundabout. From Killarney follow N22 Cork road signs and White Villa Farm finger signs from Park Road roundabout. From Kenmare take R569 via Kilgarvan to the N22, or N71 to Killarney, then the N22 Cork road. GPS: 52.04724, -9.45358

### Charges guide

| Per unit incl. 2 persons | € 22,00 - € 23,00 |
| --- | --- |
| extra person | € 6,00 |
| child | € 3,00 |

No credit cards.

# Camping Kohnenhof

Maison 1, L-9838 Obereisenbach
t: **929 464**  e: **kohnenhof@pt.lu**
alanrogers.com/LU7680  www.campingkohnenhof.lu

**Accommodation:** ☑Pitch ☑Mobile home/chalet ☐ Hotel/B&B ☐ Apartment

Nestling in a valley with the River Our running through it, Camping Kohnenhof offers a very agreeable location for a relaxing family holiday. From the minute you stop at the reception you are assured of a warm and friendly welcome. Numerous paths cross through the wooded hillside so this could be a haven for walkers. A little wooden ferry crosses the small river across the border to Germany. The river is shallow and safe for children (parental supervision essential). A large sports field and play area with a selection of equipment caters for younger campers. During the high season, an entertainment programme is organised for parents and children. The owner organises special golf weeks with games on different courses (contact the site for details). The restaurant is part of an old farmhouse and, with its open fire to keep it warm, offers a wonderful ambience to enjoy a meal. Discounts have been agreed at several local golf courses and special golfing holidays are arranged.

## Special offers
Special fishing arrangements in 2011. For more information please go to the website: www.campingkohnenhof.lu.

## You might like to know
Fishing available on site on the kilometre-long stretch of river. Fishponds and fishing shops in the vicinity. From 2011 fishing tournaments are to be held here.

☑ Coarse fishing
☐ Fly fishing
☐ Sea fishing
☐ Lake on site
☑ River on site
☐ Lake nearby (max 5km)
☐ River nearby (max 5km)
☑ Licence / permit required
☑ Equipment hire available
☐ Bait and fishing supplies

**Facilities:** Heated sanitary block with showers and washbasins in cabins. Motorcaravan service point. Laundry. Bar, restaurant, takeaway. Games and TV room. Baker calls daily. Sports field with play equipment. Boules. Bicycle hire. Golf weeks. Discounts on six local 18-hole golf courses. WiFi. Off site: Bus to Clervaux and Vianden stops (4 times daily) outside site entrance. Riding 5 km. Castle at Vianden 14 km. Monastery at Clervaux 14 km. Golf 15 km.

**Open:** 15 March - 10 November.

**Directions:** Take N7 north from Diekirch. At Hosingen, turn right onto the narrow and winding CR324 signed Eisenbach. Follow site signs from Eisenbach or Obereisenbach.
GPS: 50.01602, 6.13600

**Charges guide**

| Per unit incl. 2 persons and electricity | € 19,90 - € 28,00 |
| --- | --- |
| extra person | € 4,00 |
| dog | € 3,00 |

# Kawan Village Koningshof

Elsgeesterweg 8, NL-2231 NW Rijnsburg (Zuid-Holland)
t: 0714 026 051  e: info@koningshofholland.nl
alanrogers.com/NL5630  www.koningshofholland.nl

**Accommodation:** ☑Pitch ☑Mobile home/chalet ☐ Hotel/B&B ☐ Apartment

This popular site is run in a personal and friendly way. The 200 pitches for touring units (some with hardstandings for larger units) are laid out in groups of four or twelve, divided by hedges and trees and all with electrical connections (10A). Cars are mostly parked in areas around the perimeter and 100 static caravans, confined to one section of the site, are entirely unobtrusive. Reception, a pleasant, good quality restaurant, bar and a snack bar are grouped around a courtyard style entrance which is decorated with seasonal flowers. The site has a small outdoor, heated pool (13.5 x 7 m), with a separate paddling pool and imaginative children's play equipment. Recent additions are a recreation hall, an indoor swimming pool and a unique children's play pool with water streams, locks and play materials. The site has a number of regular British visitors from club connections who receive a friendly welcome, with English spoken. Used by tour operators (25 pitches). A very useful local information booklet (in English) is provided for visitors. A member of the Holland Tulip Parcs group.

## You might like to know
Why not visit the city of Amsterdam, just 30 km. from the campsite?

☑ Coarse fishing
☐ Fly fishing
☐ Sea fishing
☑ Lake on site
☐ River on site
☐ Lake nearby (max 5 km)
☐ River nearby (max 5 km)
☐ Licence / permit required
☐ Equipment hire available
☐ Bait and fishing supplies

**Facilities:** Three good toilet blocks, two with underfloor heating, with washbasins in cabins and provision for disabled visitors. Laundry facilities. Motorcaravan services. Gas supplies. Shop (1/4-15/10). Bar (1/4-1/11). Restaurant (1/4-10/9). Snacks and takeaway (1/4-1/11). Small outdoor pool (unsupervised; 15/5-15/9). Indoor pool (1/4-1/11). Solarium. Adventure playground and sports area. Tennis. Fishing pond (free). Bicycle hire. Entertainment in high season. Room for shows. Max. 1 dog, accepted in a limited area of the site. Off site: Sandy beach 5 km. Riding or golf 5 km. Den Haag 15 km. Amsterdam 30 km.

**Open:** 1 April - 1 November.

**Directions:** From N44/A44 Den Haag - Amsterdam motorway, take exit 7 for Oegstgeest and Rijnsburg. Turn towards Rijnsburg and follow site signs.  GPS: 52.20012, 4.45623

**Charges guide**

| | |
|---|---|
| Per unit incl. 2 persons and electricity | € 29,50 - € 32,50 |

Senior citizen discounts, group rates and special packages.

NETHERLANDS – Leeuwarden

# Camping De Kleine Wielen

Groene Ster 14, NL-8926 XE Leeuwarden (Friesland)
t: 0511 431 660   e: info@dekleinewielen.nl
alanrogers.com/NL5750   www.dekleinewielen.nl

Accommodation: ☑Pitch  ☑Mobile home/chalet  ☐Hotel/B&B  ☐Apartment

Camping De Kleine Wielen (small wheels) is named after a small lake of the same name that lies in the 1,000 ha nature and recreation area of 'De Groene Ster'. The campsite is adjacent to the lake – possible activities include boating in the lake or cycling and walking around this beautiful area of forest, grassland and ponds. The site provides 480 pitches, of which 150 are for touring units. The remaining pitches are used for privately owned mobile homes. All the touring pitches have 4A electricity and many have wonderful views over the water and surrounding countryside. The position of the site next to the water (the lake is not fenced) opens up many opportunities for sailing, rowing, canoeing or windsurfing. You can follow the river leading from the lake by boat or on shore by bicycle or car as it leads through the villages and towns such as Hindeloopen, Stavoren and Dokkum. With its central Friesland location, Camping De Kleine Wielen is ideal for a taste of the real 'Friesland' culture.

## You might like to know

Boat launching possible 2 km. from the campsite.

☑ Coarse fishing
☐ Fly fishing
☐ Sea fishing
☑ Lake on site
☐ River on site
☐ Lake nearby (max 5 km)
☐ River nearby (max 5 km)
☐ Licence / permit required
☐ Equipment hire available
☐ Bait and fishing supplies

**Facilities:** Four toilet blocks provide washbasins in cabins and preset showers (coin operated). Maintenance is variable. Facilities for disabled visitors. Motorcaravan service point. Shop (1/5-30/9). Café/restaurant and snack bar (1/4-30/9). Playground. Sports pitch. Minigolf. Lake with beach. Fishing. Rowing boats. Surf boards. Extensive recreation programme in July/Aug. Off site: Golf 1 km. Boat launching 2 km. Riding 5 km.

**Open:** 1 April - 30 September.

**Directions:** From the N355 turn off east towards Leeuwarden and follow campsite signs.
GPS: 53.21650, 5.88703

**Charges guide**

| | |
|---|---|
| Per person | € 3,95 |
| child (2-12 yrs) | € 2,95 |
| pitch incl. car | € 7,25 |
| electricity (4A) | € 3,25 |

# Camping BreeBronne

Lange Heide 9, NL-5993 PB Maasbree (Limburg)
t: 0774 652 360  e: info@breebronne.nl
alanrogers.com/NL6520  www.breebronne.nl

**Accommodation:** ☑Pitch ☑Mobile home/chalet ☐ Hotel/B&B ☐ Apartment

One of the top campsites in the Netherlands, BreeBronne is set around a large lake in a forest region. There are 370 pitches, of which 220 are for touring units. These are at least 100 m² in size and all have electricity (10A), water, waste water and cable TV connections. The touring pitches are placed in separate areas from the static units and some pitch areas are kept for people without dogs. The lake provides a sandy beach with a water slide and opportunities for swimming, sailing and windsurfing. Alternatively, you can swim in the heated open air pool or the 'sub-tropical' heated indoor pool with its special children's area. Possible excursions from the site might include a visit to Arcen, beside the Maas river, with its Schloss garden and the nearby naturally heated thermal bath. There are boat trips on the Maas. Shopping in Venlo is good with its Saturday morning market. Member of Leading Campings Group.

## You might like to know

Limburg's climate is one of the best in the Netherlands and they claim to have three times more sun than the other parts of the Netherlands.

☑ Coarse fishing
☐ Fly fishing
☐ Sea fishing
☑ Lake on site
☐ River on site
☐ Lake nearby (max 5 km)
☐ River nearby (max 5 km)
☐ Licence / permit required
☐ Equipment hire available
☐ Bait and fishing supplies

**Facilities:** The sanitary facilities are top class with a special section for children, decorated in fairy tale style, and excellent provision for disabled visitors and seniors. Launderette. Dog shower. Solarium. Private bathrooms for hire. Shop (1/4-31/10). Bar and 'De Bron' restaurant with regional specialities (all year). Takeaway. Outdoor swimming pool (15/5-1/10). Indoor pool with area for children (all year). Play area. Play room. Internet. Tennis. Animation. Fishing. Bicycle hire. Max. 1 dog. Off site: Fishing 2 km. Golf and riding 5 km. Walking in the National Parks.

**Open:** All year.

**Directions:** BreeBronne is 8 km. west of Venlo. From autobahn A67 towards Eindhoven take exit 38 and head south on the 277 road. After 3 km. fork right for Maasbree, then left (Maasbree) on the 275. At roundabout in Maasbree take third exit (site signed). Go through town and turn right after 2 km. to site 1 km. on left.
GPS: 51.36665, 6.04166

### Charges guide

| Per unit incl. 4 persons | € 28,50 - € 46,60 |
| --- | --- |
| extra person | € 4,90 |
| dog | € 5,50 |
| private bathroom | € 12,00 |

NETHERLANDS – Brielle

# Camping De Krabbeplaat

Oude Veerdam 4, NL-3231 NC Brielle (Zuid-Holland)
t: 0181 412 363  e: info@krabbeplaat.nl
alanrogers.com/NL6980  www.krabbeplaat.nl

**Accommodation:** ☑Pitch  ☑Mobile home/chalet  ☐ Hotel/B&B  ☐ Apartment

Camping de Krabbeplaat is a family run site situated near the ferry port in a wooded recreation area next to the Brielse Meer lake. There are 510 spacious pitches, with 100 for touring units, 68 with electricity (10A), cable connections and a water supply nearby. A separate field is used for groups of up to 450 guests. A nature conservation plan exists to ensure the site fits into with its natural environment. The lake and its beaches provide the perfect spot for watersports and relaxation and the site has its own harbour where you can moor your own boat. The beach is 7 km. from the site for those who prefer the sea. Plenty of cultural opportunities can be found in the historic towns of the area. Because of the large range of amenities and the tranquil nature of the site, De Krabbeplaat is perfect for families and couples.

## You might like to know

There is a large recreational lake here, where, as well as fishing, you can enjoy swimming, sailing, canoeing, pedal boating – or just walking along the water's edge. Sea fishing trips possible.

☑ Coarse fishing
☐ Fly fishing
☐ Sea fishing
☑ Lake on site
☐ River on site
☐ Lake nearby (max 5 km)
☐ River nearby (max 5 km)
☐ Licence / permit required
☐ Equipment hire available
☐ Bait and fishing supplies

**Facilities:** One large and two smaller heated toilet blocks in traditional style provide separate toilets, showers and washing cabins. High standards of cleanliness, a dedicated unit for disabled visitors and provision for babies. Warm water is free of charge. Launderette. Motorcaravan services. Supermarket and snack bar (1/4-1/10). Restaurant (July/Aug). Recreation room. Youth centre. Tennis. Playground and play field. Animal farm. Bicycle and children's pedal bike hire. Canoe, surf, pedal boat and boat hire. Fishing. WiFi. Two cottages for hikers. Dogs are not accepted.

**Open:** 27 March - 25 October.

**Directions:** From the Amsterdam direction take the A4 (Europoort), then the A15 (Europoort). Take exit for Brielle on N57 and, just before Brielle, site is signed.  GPS: 51.9097, 4.18536

**Charges 2011**

| Per unit incl. 2 persons and electricity | € 17,00 - € 23,50 |
| --- | --- |
| extra person | € 3,20 |
| child (under 12 yrs) | € 2,70 |

# Camping Wulfener Hals

Wulfener Hals Weg, D-23769 Wulfen auf Fehmarn (Schleswig-Holstein)

t: 043 718 6280   e: camping@wulfenerhals.de

alanrogers.com/DE3003   www.wulfenerhals.de

**Accommodation:** ☑Pitch ☑Mobile home/chalet ☐ Hotel/B&B ☐ Apartment

If you are travelling to Denmark or on to Sweden, taking the E47/A1 then B207 from Hamburg, and the ferry from Puttgarden to Rødbyhavn, this is a top class all year round site, either to rest overnight or as a base for a longer stay. Attractively situated by the sea, it is a large, mature site (34 hectares) and is well maintained. It has over 800 individual pitches of up to 160 m² (half for touring) in glades and some separated by bushes, with shade in the older parts, less in the newer areas nearer the sea. There are many hardstandings and 552 pitches have electricity, water and drainage. A separate area has been developed for motorcaravans. It provides 60 extra large pitches, all with electricity, water and drainage, and some with TV aerial points, together with a new toilet block. There is much to do for young and old alike at Wulfener Hals, with a new heated outdoor pool and paddling pool (unsupervised), although the sea is naturally popular as well. The site also has many sporting facilities including its own golf courses and schools for watersports. A member of Leading Campings Group.

## You might like to know

A great choice for a holiday by the sea, a short hop to a sandy beach and very high quality recreational facilities.

- ☑ Coarse fishing
- ☐ Fly fishing
- ☑ Sea fishing
- ☐ Lake on site
- ☐ River on site
- ☐ Lake nearby (max 5 km)
- ☑ River nearby (max 5 km)
- ☑ Licence / permit required
- ☐ Equipment hire available
- ☐ Bait and fishing supplies

**Facilities:** Five heated sanitary buildings have first class facilities including showers and both open washbasins and private cabins. Family bathrooms for rent. Facilities for disabled visitors. Laundry. Motorcaravan services. Shop, bar, restaurants and takeaway (April-Oct). Swimming pool (May-Oct). Sauna. Solarium. Jacuzzi. Sailing, windsurfing and diving schools. Boat slipway. Golf courses (18-hole, par 72 and 9-hole, par 27). Riding. Fishing. Archery. Good play equipment for younger children. Bicycle hire. Catamaran hire. Off site: Naturist beach 500 m. Shop 2 km.

**Open:** All year.

**Directions:** From Hamburg take A1/E47 north to Puttgarden, cross the bridge onto the island of Fehmarn and turn right twice to Avendorf and follow the signs for Wulfen and the site. GPS: 54.40805, 11.17374

**Charges guide**

| Per unit incl. 2 persons and electricity | € 13,30 - € 44,40 |
| --- | --- |
| extra person | € 3,90 - € 8,40 |
| child (2-13 yrs) | € 2,30 - € 5,70 |
| child (14-18 yrs) | € 3,40 - € 7,30 |
| dog | € 1,00 |

# Erholungszentrum Grav-Insel

Grav-Insel 1, D-46487 Wesel (North Rhine-Westphalia)
t: 028 197 2830   e: info@grav-insel.com
alanrogers.com/DE3202   www.grav-insel.de

Accommodation: ☑Pitch  ☑Mobile home/chalet  ☐ Hotel/B&B  ☐ Apartment

Grav-Insel claims to be the largest family camping site in Germany, providing entertainment and activities to match, with over 2,000 permanent units. A section for 500 touring units runs beside the water to the left of the entrance and this area has been completely renewed. These pitches, all with 10A electricity, are flat, grassy, mostly without shade and of about 100 m². A walk through the site takes you past a nature reserve and to the Rhine where you can watch the barges. Despite its size, this site is very well maintained, calm, clean and spacious and this is down to the family which started it 40 years ago. This site, on the border with Holland, is an excellent stop over for the north and east of Germany. However, once here, you may decide to stay longer to take advantage of the excellent restaurant (special evenings each week), bird watching on the private reserve or to visit Xanten with its Roman amphitheatre in the archaeological park.

## You might like to know

Grav Insel is Germanys largest campsite and offers a wide range of activities.

☑ Coarse fishing
☐ Fly fishing
☐ Sea fishing
☐ Lake on site
☐ River on site
☐ Lake nearby (max 5 km)
☑ River nearby (max 5 km)
☐ Licence / permit required
☐ Equipment hire available
☐ Bait and fishing supplies

**Facilities:** Excellent sanitary facilities, all housed in a modern building above which is the bar/restaurant (open all year). Touring area augmented by portacabin units to be renewed. Facilities for disabled visitors. Baby room. Launderette. Motorcaravan service point. Large supermarket. Entertainment area with satellite TV. WiFi. Solarium. Large play area on sand plus wet weather indoor area. Boat park. Sailing. Fishing. Swimming. Football (coaching in high season). Animation in high season. Off site: Bus service 500 m. The attractive town of Xanten 23 km. Nord Park Duisburg 25 km.

**Open:** All year.

**Directions:** Site is 5 km. northwest of Wesel. From the A3 take exit 6 and B58 towards Wesel, then right towards Rees. Turn left at sign for Flüren, through Flüren and left to site after 1.5 km. If approaching Wesel from the west (B58), cross the Rhine, turn left at first traffic lights and follow signs Grav-Insel and Flüren. GPS: 51.67062, 6.55600

### Charges guide

| | |
|---|---|
| Per person | € 2,00 - € 3,00 |
| child (under 12 yrs) | € 1,00 - € 1,50 |
| pitch | € 3,00 - € 6,50 |
| electricity | € 3,00 |

# Camping Clausensee

D-67714 Waldfischbach-Burgalben (Rhineland Palatinate)
t: 063 335 744  e: info@campingclausensee.de
alanrogers.com/DE3259  www.campingclausensee.de

Accommodation: ☑Pitch  ☑Mobile home/chalet  ☐Hotel/B&B  ☐Apartment

Clausensee is a well equipped family site on the banks of an attractive lake with a wide grassy bank. This site is open all year. Pitches are grassy with varying degrees of shade. Most pitches have electricity. A number of special motorcravan pitches are provided and a discounted overnight rate is available (arrivals after 19.00 and departures before 10.00). A number of fully equipped chalets, caravans or bungalow tents are available for rent. The lake is the focal point of the site with pedaloes and rowing boats for hire. It is also popular with fishermen (permit required – available on site). Clausensee lies at the heart of the Pfälzerwald (Palatinate Forest), a vast area of natural beauty, and one of the biggest forests in Europe. The German wine route extends along the eastern side of the forest, bordering the Upper Rhine Valley. The Vosges mountains in France rise to the south. This is excellent cycling and walking country with hundreds of kilometres of waymarked trails. The Mountainbike Park Pfälzerwald was added in 2005.

## Special offers
Day passes, weekly passes, annual passes.
Fishing from shore or by boat.

## You might like to know
There is a ten-acre lake, nestled in the picturesque setting of Pfälzerwald (Palatinate Forest), an anglers paradise.

☑ Coarse fishing
☐ Fly fishing
☐ Sea fishing
☑ Lake on site
☐ River on site
☐ Lake nearby (max 5 km)
☐ River nearby (max 5 km)
☑ Licence / permit required
☐ Equipment hire available
☐ Bait and fishing supplies

**Facilities:** Shop. Bar. Restaurant. Takeaway meals. Direct access to lake (suitable for swimming). Pedaloes and rowing boats. Fishing. Bicycle hire. Play area. Tourist information. Caravans, equipped tents and chalets for rent. Off site: Golf (discounts available for campers). Walking and cycling. German wine route.

**Open:** All year.

**Directions:** Approaching from the A6 Kaiserslautern-Mannheim, motorway, leave at exit 15 (Kaiserslautern-West) and join B270 towards Waldfischbach-Burgalben. From Waldfischbach-Burgalben follow signs to the site for 7 km. (towards Clausen). GPS: 49.27544, 7.720116

### Charges guide

| Per unit incl. 2 persons and electricity | € 22,50 - € 25,50 |
| --- | --- |
| extra person | € 7,00 |
| child (under 13 yrs) | € 3,70 |
| dog | € 4,20 |

# Camping & Ferienpark Teichmann

Zum Träumen 1A, D-34516 Vöhl-Herzhausen (Hessen)
t: 056 352 45  e: camping-teichmann@t-online.de
alanrogers.com/DE3280  www.camping-teichmann.de

Accommodation: ☑Pitch ☑Mobile home/chalet ☐Hotel/B&B ☐Apartment

Situated near the eastern end of the 27 km. long Edersee and the National Park Kellerwald-Edersee, this attractively set site is surrounded by wooded hills and encircles a six hectare lake which has separate areas for swimming, fishing and boating. Of the 460 pitches, 250 are touring, all with 10A electricity and 50 with fresh and waste water connections. The pitches are on level grass, some having an area of hardstanding, and are separated by hedges and mature trees. At the far side of the lake from the entrance is a separate area for tents with its own sanitary block. The adjoining national park, a popular leisure region, offers a wealth of holiday/sporting activities including walking, cycling, (there are two passenger ferries that take cycles) boat trips, cable car and much more, full details are available at the friendly reception. For winter sport lovers the ski centre at Winterberg is only 30 km. away from this all year round site. With a wide range of facilities for children this is an ideal family site as well as being suited to country lovers who can enjoy the endless forest and lakeside walks/cycle tracks in the park.

## You might like to know
At low water, in late summer, during dry years, the usually submerged remnants of the three villages of Asel, Bringhausen, and Berich, along with a bridge across the original river bed, can all be seen.

☑ Coarse fishing
☐ Fly fishing
☐ Sea fishing
☑ Lake on site
☐ River on site
☐ Lake nearby (max 5 km)
☐ River nearby (max 5 km)
☐ Licence / permit required
☐ Equipment hire available
☐ Bait and fishing supplies

**Facilities:** Three good quality sanitary blocks can be heated and have free showers, washbasins (open and in cabins), baby rooms and facilities for wheelchair users. Laundry. Motorcaravan services. Café and shop (both summer only). Restaurant by entrance open all day (closed Feb). Watersports. Boat and bicycle hire. Lake swimming. Fishing. Minigolf. Tennis. Playground. Sauna. Solarium. Disco (high season). Internet access. Off site: New National Park opposite site entrance. Riding 500 m. Golf 25 km. Cable car (you can take bikes). Aquapark. Boat trips on the Edersee.

**Open:** All year.

**Directions:** Site is 45 km. from Kassel. From A44 Oberhausen - Kassel autobahn, take exit 64 for Diemelstadt and head south for Korbach. Site is between Korbach and Frankenberg on the B252 road, 1 km. to the south of Herzhausen at the pedestrian traffic lights.
GPS: 51.17550, 8.89067

**Charges guide**

| | |
|---|---|
| Per unit incl. 2 persons and electricity | € 25,00 - € 29,00 |

# Camping Elbsee

Am Elbsee 3, D-87648 Aitrang (Bavaria (S))
t: 083 432 48  e: camping@elbsee.de
alanrogers.com/DE3672  www.elbsee.de

**Accommodation:** ☑Pitch ☑Mobile home/chalet ☑Hotel/B&B ☐ Apartment

This attractive site, with its associated hotel and restaurant about 400 m. away, lies on land sloping down to the lake. This is not an area well known to tourists, although the towns of Marktoberdorf (14 km), Kaufbeuren (16 km) and Kempten (21 km) merit a visit. With this in mind, the owners have set about providing good facilities and a developing program of activities. All the 120 touring pitches have access to electricity (16A) and 78 also have their own water supply and waste water outlet. Some of the pitches (those restricted to tents) slope slightly. In high season there are organised outings, musical performances on site or at the hotel, painting courses and activities for children. Next to the site is a supervised lake bathing area, operated by the municipality, with a kiosk selling drinks and snacks, a playground and an indoor play area. Entrance to this is at a reduced price for campers.

## You might like to know
This site is open all year – maybe a good choice for a winter break.

- ☑ Coarse fishing
- ☐ Fly fishing
- ☐ Sea fishing
- ☑ Lake on site
- ☐ River on site
- ☐ Lake nearby (max 5 km)
- ☐ River nearby (max 5 km)
- ☑ Licence / permit required
- ☐ Equipment hire available
- ☐ Bait and fishing supplies

**Facilities:** Two clean, well appointed, heated sanitary blocks include free showers, washbasins all in cabins, a children's bathroom and family bathrooms to rent. Facilities for disabled visitors. Dog shower. Motorcaravan service point. Shop (order bread for following day). New playground, indoor play area and activity rooms. TV, games and meeting rooms. Sports field. Fishing. Bicycle hire. Riding. Boat launching. Activity programme (20/7-31/8). Off site: At hotel, very good restaurant, takeaway and bar. Shop and ATM point 2 km. Golf 12 km.

**Open:** All year.

**Directions:** From centre of Marktoberdorf, take minor road northwest to Ruderatshofen and from there take minor road west towards Aitrang. Just south of Aitrang, site is signed to south of the road. The road to the site (2 km) is winding and narrow, but two caravans can just about pass. GPS: 47.80277, 10.55343

**Charges guide**

| Per unit incl. 2 persons and electricity (per kWh) | € 21,90 - € 24,00 |
| --- | --- |
| extra person | € 6,20 |
| child (4-15 yrs) | € 3,00 |
| dog | € 4,00 |

# Kur & Feriencamping Dreiquellenbad

Singham 40, D-94086 Bad Griesbach (Bavaria (S))
t: 085 329 6130   e: info@camping-bad-griesbach.de
alanrogers.com/DE3697   www.camping-bad-griesbach.de

Accommodation: ☑Pitch  ☑Mobile home/chalet  ☐Hotel/B&B  ☐Apartment

This site is to the southwest of Passau, a town which dates back to Roman times and lies on a peninsula between the rivers Danube and Inn. Dreiquellenbad is an exceptional site in a quiet rural area, with 200 pitches, all of which are used for touring units. All pitches have electricity, water, waste water and TV points. English is spoken at reception which also houses a shop and good tourist information. A luxury leisure complex includes indoor and outdoor thermal pools, a sauna, Turkish bath and jacuzzi (the use of which is free to campers). An adjoining building provides various beauty and complementary health treatments. A member of Leading Campings Group.

## You might like to know
Bad Griesbach thermal spa is the perfect place to escape from the daily grind, a place where you can restore your balance and physical wellbeing, and replenish your positive energy.

- ☑ Coarse fishing
- ☐ Fly fishing
- ☐ Sea fishing
- ☐ Lake on site
- ☐ River on site
- ☐ Lake nearby (max 5 km)
- ☑ River nearby (max 5 km)
- ☑ Licence / permit required
- ☐ Equipment hire available
- ☐ Bait and fishing supplies

**Facilities:** Excellent sanitary facilities include private cabins and free showers, facilities for disabled visitors, special child facilities and a dog shower. Two private bathrooms for rent. Laundry facilities. Bar/restaurant. Motorcaravan services. Shop. Gym. Luxury leisure complex. Play area. Bicycle hire. Fishing. Internet. WiFi. Off site: Golf 2 km. Spa facilities of Bad Griesbach within walking distance.

**Open:** All year.

**Directions:** Site is 15 km. from the A3. Take exit 118 and follow signs for Pocking. After 2 km. turn right on B388. Site is in the hamlet of Singham - turn right into Karpfhan then left towards site. GPS: 48.42001, 13.19261

**Charges guide**

| Per unit incl. 2 persons | |
|---|---|
| and electricity | € 10,90 - € 11,90 |
| extra person | € 7,30 |
| child (0-14 yrs) | € 4,50 |
| dog | € 2,30 |

# Camping Havelberge am Woblitzsee

An de Havelberg 1, D-17237 Userin/Ot Gross Quassau (Mecklenburg-West Pomerania)
t: **039 812 4790**  e: **info@haveltourist.de**
alanrogers.com/DE3820  www.haveltourist.de

**Accommodation:** ☑Pitch  ☑Mobile home/chalet  ☐ Hotel/B&B  ☐ Apartment

The Müritz National Park is a very large area of lakes and marshes, popular for birdwatching as well as watersports, and Havelberge is a large, well equipped site to use as a base for enjoying the area. It is quite steep in places here with many terraces, most with shade, less in newer areas, with views over the lake. There are 400 pitches in total with 330 good sized, numbered touring pitches, most with 16A electrical connections and 230 pitches on a newly developed area to the rear of the site with water and drainage. Pitches on the new field are level and separated by low hedges and bushes but have no shade. Over 170 seasonal pitches with a number of attractive chalets and an equal number of mobile homes are in a separate area. In the high season this is a busy park with lots going on to entertain families of all ages, whilst in the low seasons this is a peaceful base for exploring an unspoilt area of nature. A member of Leading Campings Group.

## Special offers
Angling cards and (if necessary) tourist fishing licences are available at reception.

## You might like to know
Max. two rods per fishing permit. Night fishing available. Motor boats (up to 5hp) can be hired. Boat fishing allowed only at anchor.

☑ **Coarse fishing**
☐ **Fly fishing**
☐ **Sea fishing**
☑ **Lake on site**
☑ **River on site**
☐ **Lake nearby (max 5 km)**
☐ **River nearby (max 5 km)**
☑ **Licence / permit required**
☐ **Equipment hire available**
☑ **Bait and fishing supplies**

**Facilities:** Four sanitary buildings (one new and of a very high standard) provide very good facilities, with private cabins, showers on payment and large section for children. Fully equipped kitchen and laundry. Motorcaravan service point. Small shop and modern restaurant (April-Oct). The lake provides fishing, swimming from a small beach and boats can be launched (over 5 hp requires a German boat licence). Canoes, rowing boats, windsurfers and bikes can be hired. Play areas and entertainment in high season. Internet access. Off site: Riding 3.5 km.

**Open:** All year.

**Directions:** From A19 Rostock - Berlin road take exit 18 and follow B198 to Wesenberg and go left to Klein Quassow and follow site signs. GPS: 53.30517, 13.00133

**Charges guide**

| Per unit incl. 2 persons and electricity | € 15,30 - € 31,50 |
| --- | --- |
| extra person | € 4,00 - € 6,50 |
| child (2-14 yrs) | € 1,50 - € 4,30 |
| dog | € 1,00 - € 4,30 |

# Camping & Freizeitpark LuxOase

Arnsdorfer Strasse 1, Kleinröhrsdorf, D-01900 Dresden (Saxony)
t: 035 952 56666  e: info@luxoase.de
alanrogers.com/DE3833  www.luxoase.de

**Accommodation:** ☑Pitch ☑Mobile home/chalet ☐Hotel/B&B ☐Apartment

This is a well organised and quiet site located just north of Dresden with easy access from the autobahn. The site has very good facilities and is arranged on grassland beside a lake. There is access from the site to the lake through a gate. Although the site is fairly open, trees do provide shade in some areas. There are 138 large touring pitches (plus 50 seasonal in a separate area), marked by bushes or posts on generally flat or slightly sloping grass. All have 10/16A electricity and 100 have water and drainage. At the entrance is an area of hardstanding (with electricity) for late arrivals. The main entrance building houses the amenities and in front of the building is some very modern play equipment on bark. You may swim, fish or use inflatables in the lake. A wide animation program is organised for children in high season. There are many interesting places to visit apart from Dresden and Meissen, with the fascinating National Park Sächsische Schweiz (Saxon Switzerland) on the border with the Czech Republic offering some spectacular scenery. A member of Leading Campings Group.

## You might like to know

A number of coach trips are on offer here – including weekly day-trips to Prague, a sight-seeing excursion through Dresden and a trip to the castle of Pillnitz with a steam riverboat-trip through the Saxony countryside.

☑ Coarse fishing
☐ Fly fishing
☐ Sea fishing
☑ Lake on site
☐ River on site
☐ Lake nearby (max 5 km)
☐ River nearby (max 5 km)
☑ Licence / permit required
☐ Equipment hire available
☐ Bait and fishing supplies

**Facilities:** A well equipped building provides modern, heated facilities with private cabins, a family room, baby room, units for disabled visitors and two bathrooms for hire. Jacuzzi. Kitchen. Gas supplies. Motorcaravan services. Shop. Bar and restaurant (March-Nov). Bicycle hire. Lake swimming. Sports field. Fishing. Play area. Sauna. Train, bus and theatre tickets from reception. Internet point. WiFi. Minigolf. Fitness room. Regular guided bus trips to Dresden, Prague etc. Off site: Riding next door (lessons available). Public transport to Dresden 1 km. Golf 7.5 km. Nearby zoo and indoor karting etc.

**Open:** 1 March - 7 November (phone in winter).

**Directions:** Site is 17 km. northeast of Dresden. From the A4 (Dresden - Görlitz) take exit 85 (Pulnitz) and travel south towards Radeberg. Pass through Leppersdorf and site is signed to the left. Follow signs for Kleinröhrsdorf and camping. Site is 4 km. from the autobahn exit. GPS: 51.120401, 13.980103

### Charges guide

| | |
|---|---|
| Per person | € 5,00 - € 7,50 |
| child (3-15 yrs) | € 2,55 - € 4,50 |
| pitch | € 7,50 - € 10,00 |
| electricity | € 2,60 - € 2,90 |

# Holiday Park Lisci Farma

Dolni Branna 350, CZ-54362 Vrchlabi (Vychodocesky)
t: **499 421 473**  e: **info@liscifarma.cz**
alanrogers.com/CZ4590  www.liscifarma.cz

**Accommodation:** ☑Pitch  ☑Mobile home/chalet  ☑Hotel/B&B  ☐ Apartment

This is truly an excellent site that could be in Western Europe considering its amenities, pitches and welcome. However, Lisci Farma retains a pleasant Czech atmosphere. In the winter months, when local skiing is available, snow chains are essential. The 260 pitches are fairly flat, although the terrain is slightly sloping and some pitches are terraced. There is shade and some pitches have hardstanding. The site is well equipped for the whole family to enjoy with its adventure playground offering trampolines for children, archery, beach volleyball, Russian bowling and an outdoor bowling court for older youngsters. A beautiful sandy, lakeside beach is 800 m. from the entrance. The more active amongst you can go paragliding or rock climbing, with experienced people to guide you. This site is very suitable for relaxing or exploring the culture of the area. Excursions to Prague are organised. The site reports the addition of completely new electrical connections, a restaurant, games room and mini-market.

## You might like to know

Prague can easily be reached from Lisci Farma and makes a wonderful day trip.

☑ **Coarse fishing**
☐ Fly fishing
☐ Sea fishing
☐ Lake on site
☐ River on site
☑ **Lake nearby (max 5 km)**
☐ River nearby (max 5 km)
☑ **Licence / permit required**
☐ Equipment hire available
☐ Bait and fishing supplies

**Facilities:** Two good sanitary blocks, one new in 2005 near the entrance and another modern block next to the hotel, both include toilets, washbasins and spacious, controllable showers (on payment). Child size toilets and baby room. Toilet for disabled visitors. Sauna and massage. Launderette with sinks, hot water and a washing machine. Shop (15/6-15/9). Bar/snack bar with pool table. Games room. Swimming pool (6x12 m). Adventure style playground on grass with climbing wall. Trampolines. Tennis. Minigolf. Archery. Russian bowling. Paragliding. Rock climbing. Bicycle hire. Animation programme. Excursions to Prague. Off site: Fishing and beach 800 m. Riding 2 km. Golf 5 km.

**Open:** 1 December - 31 March and 1 May - 31 October.

**Directions:** Follow road no. 14 from Liberec to Vrchlabi. At the roundabout turn in the direction of Prague and site is about 1 km. on the right. GPS: 50.61036, 15.60264

### Charges guide

| Per unit incl. 2 persons and electricity | CZK 417 - 800 |
| --- | --- |
| extra person | CZK 75 - 115 |
| child (5-12 yrs) | CZK 59 - 90 |
| dog | CZK 59 - 90 |

# Camping Frymburk

Frymburk 184, CZ-38279 Frymburk (Jihocesky)
t: **380 735 284**  e: **info@campingfrymburk.cz**
alanrogers.com/CZ4720  www.campingfrymburk.cz

**Accommodation:** ☑Pitch  ☑Mobile home/chalet  ☐ Hotel/B&B  ☐ Apartment

Camping Frymburk is beautifully located on the Lipno lake in southern Bohemia and is an ideal site. From this site, activities could include walking, cycling, swimming, sailing, canoeing or rowing and afterwards you could relax in the small, cosy bar/restaurant. You could enjoy a real Czech meal in one of the restaurants in Frymburk or on site. The site has 170 level pitches on terraces (all with 6A electricity, some with hardstanding and 4 have private sanitary units) and from the lower terraces on the edge of the lake there are lovely views over the water to the woods on the opposite side. A ferry crosses the lake from Frymburk where one can walk or cycle in the woods. The Dutch owner, Mr Wilzing, will welcome the whole family, personally siting your caravan. Children will be entertained by 'Kidstown' and the site has a small beach.

## You might like to know

Camping Frymburk is situated on Lake Lipno in Southern Bohemia, the largest protected nature area in the Czech Republic and which boasts a mountain range over 120 km. long.

- ☑ **Coarse fishing**
- ☐ **Fly fishing**
- ☐ **Sea fishing**
- ☑ **Lake on site**
- ☐ **River on site**
- ☐ **Lake nearby (max 5 km)**
- ☑ **River nearby (max 5 km)**
- ☑ **Licence / permit required**
- ☐ **Equipment hire available**
- ☐ **Bait and fishing supplies**

**Facilities:** Three immaculate toilet blocks with toilets, washbasins, preset showers on payment and an en-suite bathroom with toilet, basin and shower. Facilities for disabled visitors. Launderette. Restaurant and bar (10/5-15/9). Motorcaravan services. Canoe, bicycle, pedalos, rowing boat and surfboard hire. Kidstown. Volleyball competitions. Rafting. Bus trips to Prague. Torches useful. Internet access and WiFi. Off site: Shops and restaurants in the village 900 m. from reception. Golf 7 km. Riding 20 km.

**Open:** 30 April - 1 October.

**Directions:** Take exit 114 at Passau in Germany (near the Austrian border) towards Freyung in the Czech Republic. Continue on this road till Philipsreut and from there follow the no. 4 road towards Vimperk. Turn right a few kilometres after the border towards Volary on no. 141 road. From Volary follow the no. 163 road to Horni Plana, Cerna and Frymburk. Site is on the 163 road, right after the village.
GPS: 48.655947, 14.170239

**Charges guide**

| Per unit incl. 2 persons and electricity | CZK 460 - 620 |
|---|---|
| extra person | CZK 70 - 100 |
| child (under 12 yrs) | CZK 50 - 70 |

No credit cards.

# Camping Bucek

Tratice 170, CZ-27101 Nové Straseci (Stredocesky)
t: 313 564 212  e: info@campingbucek.cz
alanrogers.com/CZ4825  www.campingbucek.cz

**Accommodation:** ☑Pitch ☑Mobile home/chalet ☐ Hotel/B&B ☐ Apartment

Camping Bucek is a pleasant Dutch owned site 40 km. west of Prague. Its proprietors also own Camping Frymburk (CZ4720). Bucek is located on the edge of woodland and has direct access to a small lake – canoes and rowing boats are available for hire, as well as sun loungers on the site's private beach. There are 100 pitches here, many with pleasant views over the lake, and all with electrical connections (6A). Shade is quite limited. Nearby, Revnicov is a pleasant small town with a range of shops and restaurants. The castles of Karlstejn and Krivoklát are also within easy access, along with Karlovy Vary and Prague itself.

## You might like to know

Camping Bucek extends over five hectares, including one hectare of forest. It has direct access to a large lake.

- ☑ Coarse fishing
- ☐ Fly fishing
- ☐ Sea fishing
- ☑ Lake on site
- ☐ River on site
- ☐ Lake nearby (max 5 km)
- ☐ River nearby (max 5 km)
- ☑ Licence / permit required
- ☐ Equipment hire available
- ☐ Bait and fishing supplies

**Facilities:** Renovated toilet blocks with free hot showers. Washing and drying machine. Direct lake access. Swimming pool. Pedaloes, canoes, lounger hire. Minigolf. Play area. Off site: Revnicov 2 km. with shops (including a supermarket), bars and restaurants. Prague 40 km. Karlovy Vary 10 km. Koniprusy caves.

**Open:** 24 April - 15 September.

**Directions:** From the west, take no. 6/E48 express road towards Prague. Site is close to this road, about 3 km. after the Revnicov exit and is clearly signed from this point. Coming from the east, ignore other camping signs and continue until Bucek is signed (to the north). GPS: 50.1728, 13.8348

### Charges guide

| | |
|---|---|
| Per unit incl. 2 persons and electricity | CZK 450 - 590 |
| extra person | CZK 75 - 95 |
| child (under 12 yrs) | CZK 50 - 60 |
| dog | CZK 50 - 60 |

Reductions in low season.
No credit cards.

# Fårup Sø Camping

Fårupvej 58, DK-7300 Jelling (Vejle)
t: 75 87 13 44  e: faarup-soe@dk-camp.dk
alanrogers.com/DK2048  www.dk-camp.dk/faarup-soe

**Accommodation:** ☑Pitch  ☑Mobile home/chalet  ☐ Hotel/B&B  ☐ Apartment

This site was originally set up in the woodlands of Jelling Skov where local farmers each had their own plot. Owned by the Dutch/Danish Albring family, this is a rural location on the Fårup Lake. Many trees have now been removed to give the site a welcoming, open feel. Fårup Sø Camping has 250 grassy pitches, mostly on terraces (from top to bottom the height difference is 53 m). The 35 newest terraced pitches provide beautiful views of the countryside and the Fårup lake. There are 200 pitches for touring units, most with 10A electricity, and some tent pitches without electricity. Next to the top toilet block is a barbecue area with a terrace and good views. A neighbour rents out water bikes and takes high season excursions onto the lake with a real Viking Ship which campers can join. During the last weekend of May the site celebrates the Jelling Musical Festival when it is advisable to book in advance. This family site is ideal for those who want to enjoy a relaxed holiday on the lakeside beaches or go walking or cycling through the surrounding countryside.

## You might like to know

The nearby Madsby play park has lots of free activities for children including an adventure playground and animal farm.

☑ **Coarse fishing**
☐ **Fly fishing**
☐ **Sea fishing**
☑ **Lake on site**
☐ **River on site**
☐ **Lake nearby (max 5 km)**
☐ **River nearby (max 5 km)**
☐ **Licence / permit required**
☐ **Equipment hire available**
☐ **Bait and fishing supplies**

**Facilities:** One modern and one older toilet block have British style toilets, open style washbasins and controllable hot showers. Family shower rooms. Baby room. Facilities for disabled visitors. Laundry. Campers' kitchen. Motorcaravan services. Shop (bread to order). Outdoor heated swimming pool (15x5 m). Whirlpool. New playgrounds. Minigolf. Games room. Pony riding. Lake with fishing, watersports and Viking ship. Activities for children (high season). Internet. Off site: Golf and riding 2 km. Lion Park 8 km. Boat launching 10 km. Legoland 20 km.

**Open:** 1 April - 30 September.

**Directions:** From Vejle take the 28 road towards Billund. In Skibet turn right towards Fårup Sø, Jennum and Jelling and follow the signs to Fårup Sô.  GPS: 55.73614, 9.41777

**Charges guide**

| Per person | DKK 61 |
| --- | --- |
| child (3-11 yrs) | DKK 35 |
| pitch | DKK 15 - 35 |
| electricity | DKK 28 |

# Fornæs Camping

Stensmarkvej 36, DK-8500 Grenå (Århus)
t: 86 33 23 30   e: fornaes@1031.inord.dk
alanrogers.com/DK2070

Accommodation: ☑Pitch  ☑Mobile home/chalet  ☐Hotel/B&B  ☐Apartment

In the grounds of a former farm, Fornæs Camping is about 5 km. from Grenå. From reception a wide, gravel access road descends through a large grassy field to the sea. Pitches to the left are mostly level, to the right slightly sloping with some terracing and views of the Kattegat. The rows of pitches are divided into separate areas by colourful bushes and each row is marked by a concrete tub containing a young tree and colourful flowers. Fornæs has 320 pitches of which 240 are for tourers, the others being used for seasonal visitors. All touring pitches have 10A electricity. At the foot of the site is a pebble beach with a large grass area behind it for play and sunbathing. There is also an attractive outdoor pool with two slides, a paddling pool, sauna, solarium and whirlpool near the entrance. Here also, a room serves as a restaurant, takeaway and bar, and in a former barn there is a games room. Fornæs is a good base from which to explore this part of Denmark or for taking the ferry to Hjelm island or to Sweden.

## You might like to know
Aarhus, Denmark's second city, is within easy reach, and has a very attractive old town.

☐ Coarse fishing
☐ Fly fishing
☑ Sea fishing
☐ Lake on site
☐ River on site
☐ Lake nearby (max 5 km)
☑ River nearby (max 5 km)
☑ Licence / permit required
☐ Equipment hire available
☐ Bait and fishing supplies

**Facilities:** Two toilet blocks have British style toilets, washbasins in cabins and controllable hot showers (on payment). Child-size toilets. Family shower rooms. Baby room. Facilities for disabled visitors. Fully equipped laundry. Campers' kitchen. Motorcaravan service point. Shop. Café/grill with bar and takeaway (evenings). Swimming pool (80 m²) with paddling pool. Sauna and solarium. Play area and adventure playground. Games room with satellite TV. Minigolf. Fishing. Watersports. Off site: Golf and riding 5 km.

**Open:** 15 March - 20 September.

**Directions:** From Århus follow the 15 road towards Grenå and then the 16 road towards town centre. Turn north and follow signs for Fornæs and the site. GPS: 56.45602, 10.94107

### Charges guide

| | |
|---|---|
| Per person | DKK 67 - 75 |
| child (1-12 yrs) | DKK 38 - 42 |
| electricity (10A) | DKK 28 |

Credit cards 5% surcharge.

# Holmens Camping

Klostervej 148, DK-8680 Ry (Århus)
t: **86 89 17 62**  e: **info@holmens-camping.dk**
alanrogers.com/DK2080  www.holmens-camping.dk

**Accommodation:** ☑Pitch ☑Mobile home/chalet ☐ Hotel/B&B ☐ Apartment

Holmens Camping lies between Silkeborg and Skanderborg in a very beautiful part of Denmark. The site is close to the waters of the Gudensø and Rye Møllesø lakes which are used for boating and canoeing. Walking and cycling are also popular activities. Holmens has 225 grass touring pitches, partly terraced and divided by young trees and shrubs. The site itself is surrounded by mature trees. Almost all the pitches have 6A electricity and vary in size between 70-100 m². A small tent field is close to the lake, mainly used by those who like to travel by canoe. The lake is suitable for swimming but the site also has an attractive pool complex. This comprises two circular pools linked by a bridge and a paddling pool with water canon. There are plenty of opportunities for activities including boat hire on the lake and fishing (the site has its own fishing pond). Both Skanderborg and Silkeborg are worth a visit and in Ry you can attend the Skt. Hans party which takes place at midsummer.

## You might like to know
Boats are available for hire on site and popular for fishing in the clear waters here.

☑ Coarse fishing
☐ Fly fishing
☐ Sea fishing
☑ Lake on site
☐ River on site
☐ Lake nearby (max 5 km)
☑ River nearby (max 5 km)
☑ Licence / permit required
☑ Equipment hire available
☐ Bait and fishing supplies

**Facilities:** One traditional and one modern toilet block have washbasins (open and in cabins) and controllable hot showers (on payment). En-suite facilities with toilet, basin, shower. Baby room. Excellent facilities for disabled visitors. Laundry. Campers' kitchen. Small shop. Covered pool with jet stream and paddling pool with water canon. Finnish sauna, solarium, massage and fitness facilities (charged). Pool bar. Extensive games room. Playground. Tennis. Minigolf. Fishing. Bicycle hire. Boat rental. Large units are not accepted. Off site: Riding 2 km. Golf 14 km.

**Open:** 16 March - 29 September.

**Directions:** Going north on E45, take exit 52 at Skanderborg turning west on 445 road towards Ry. In Ry follow the site signs.
GPS: 56.07607, 9.76549

**Charges guide**

| Per person | DKK 62 - 73 |
|---|---|
| child (3-11 yrs) | DKK 35 - 40 |
| pitch | DKK 20 |

# Odda Camping

Borsto, N-5750 Odda (Hordaland)
t: **41 32 16 10**  e: **post@oppleve.no**
alanrogers.com/NO2320  www.oppleve.no

**Accommodation:** ☑Pitch  ☑Mobile home/chalet  ☐ Hotel/B&B  ☐ Apartment

Bordered by the Folgefonna glacier to the west and the Hardangervidda plateau to the east and south, Odda is an industrial town with electro-chemical enterprises based on zinc mining and hydro-electric power. This site has been attractively developed on the town's southern outskirts. It is spread over 2.5 acres of flat, mature woodland, which is divided into small clearings by massive boulders. Access is by well tended tarmac roads which wind their way among the trees and boulders. There are 55 touring pitches including 36 with electricity. The site fills up in the evenings and can be crowded with facilities stretched from the end of June to early August. The site is just over a kilometre from the centre, on the shores of the Sandvin lake (good salmon and trout fishing) and on the minor road leading up the Buar Valley to the Buar glacier, Vidfoss Falls and Folgefonna ice cap. It is possible to walk to the ice face but in the later stages this is quite hard going! At the turn of the century, Odda was one of the most popular destinations for the European upper classes.

## You might like to know

Try canoeing on the idyllic lake Sandvinsvatnet. There are plenty of bays to paddle through. On the trip you will see a panoramic view of Buer Glacier in the west.

- ☑ Coarse fishing
- ☐ Fly fishing
- ☐ Sea fishing
- ☑ Lake on site
- ☐ River on site
- ☑ Lake nearby (max 5 km)
- ☐ River nearby (max 5 km)
- ☑ Licence / permit required
- ☑ Equipment hire available
- ☐ Bait and fishing supplies

**Facilities:** A single timber building at the entrance houses the reception office and the simple, but clean sanitary facilities which provide, for each sex, 2 WCs, one hot shower (on payment) and 3 open washbasins. A new building provides additional unisex toilets, showers and laundry facilities. Small kitchen with dishwashing facilities. Mini shop. Off site: Town facilities close.

**Open:** All year.

**Directions:** Site is on the southern outskirts of Odda, signed off road to Buar, with a well marked access.  GPS: 60.05320, 6.54380

### Charges guide

| | |
|---|---|
| Per person | NOK 10 |
| tent and car | NOK 110 |
| caravan or motorcaravan | NOK 130 |
| electricity | NOK 40 |

No credit cards.

# Lærdal Ferie & Fritidspark

Grandavegens, N-6886 Lærdal (Sogn og Fjordane)
t: 57 66 66 95   e: info@laerdalferiepark.com
alanrogers.com/NO2375   www.laerdalferiepark.com

Accommodation: ☑Pitch  ☑Mobile home/chalet  ☑Hotel/B&B  ☐ Apartment

This site is beside the famous Sognefjord, the longest fjord in the world. It is ideally situated if you want to explore the glaciers, fjords and waterfalls of the region. The 100 pitches are level with well trimmed grass and connected by tarmac roads and are suitable for tents, caravans and motorcaravans. There are 80 electrical hook-ups. The fully licensed restaurant serves traditional meals as well as snacks and pizzas. The pretty little village of Lærdal, only 400 m. away, is well worth a visit. A walk among the old, small, wooden houses is a pleasant and interesting experience. You can hire boats on the site for short trips on the fjord. Guided hiking, cycling and fishing trips are also available. The site also provides cabins, flats and rooms to rent, plus a brand new motel, all very modern and extremely tastefully designed.

## You might like to know
Wonderful fishing on the Lærdalselvi, one of Norway's most celebrated salmon rivers.

- ☑ Coarse fishing
- ☐ Fly fishing
- ☐ Sea fishing
- ☐ Lake on site
- ☑ River on site
- ☐ Lake nearby (max 5 km)
- ☑ River nearby (max 5 km)
- ☐ Licence / permit required
- ☐ Equipment hire available
- ☐ Bait and fishing supplies

**Facilities:** Two modern and well decorated sanitary blocks with washbasins (some in cubicles), showers on payment, and toilets. Facilities for disabled visitors. Children's room. Washing machine and dryer. Kitchen. Motorcaravan services. Bar, restaurant and takeaway (20/5-5/9). Small shop. TV room. Playground. Motorboats, rowing boats, canoes, bicycles and pedal cars for hire. Bicycle hire. Fishing. Internet (WiFi) at reception. Off site: Cruises on the Sognefjord 400 m. The Norwegian Wild Salmon Centre 400 m. Riding 500 m. Golf 12 km. The Flåm railway 40 km.

**Open:** All year,
by telephone request 1 Nov - 14 March.

**Directions:** Site is on road 5 (from the Oslo - Bergen road, E 16) 400 m. north of Lærdal village centre. GPS: 61.09977, 7.46962

### Charges guide

| Per unit incl. 2 persons and electricity | NOK 210 |
| --- | --- |
| extra person | NOK 50 |
| child (4-15 yrs) | NOK 25 |

# Kjørnes Camping

N-6856 Sogndal (Sogn og Fjordane)
t: **57 67 45 80**  e: **camping@kjornes.no**
alanrogers.com/NO2390  www.kjornes.no

**Accommodation:** ☑Pitch  ☑Mobile home/chalet  ☐Hotel/B&B  ☑Apartment

Kjørnes Camping is idyllically situated on the Sognefjord, 3 km. from the centre of Sogndal. It occupies a long open meadow which is terraced down to the waterside. The site has 100 pitches for camping units (all with electricity), nine cabins and two apartments for rent. Located at the very centre of the 'fjord kingdom' by the main no. 5 road, this site is the ideal base from which to explore the Sognefjord. You are within a short drive (maximum one hour) from all the major attractions including the Jostedal glacier, the Nærøyfjord, the Flåm Railway, the Urnes Stave Church and Sognefjellet. This site is ideal for those who enjoy peace and quiet, lovely scenery or a spot of fishing. Access is via a narrow lane with passing places, which drops down towards the fjord three kilometres from Sogndal.

## You might like to know

Don't miss the Jostedal Glacier, the largest on the European mainland. Glacier climbing equipment for hire! Motorboat and rowing boat hire available (5 km).

☑ **Coarse fishing**
☐ Fly fishing
☑ **Sea fishing**
☐ Lake on site
☑ **River on site**
☑ **Lake nearby (max 5 km)**
☐ River nearby (max 5 km)
☐ Licence / permit required
☐ Equipment hire available
☐ Bait and fishing supplies

**Facilities:** A new, high quality sanitary building was added in 2008. Baby room. Facilities for disabled visitors. A new building provides a kitchen with cooking facilities, dishwasher, a dining area overlooking the fjord, and laundry facilities. Small shop (20/6-20/8). Satellite TV, WiFi and internet. Off site: Hiking, glacier walks, climbing, rafting, walking around Sognefjord. Details from reception. Bicycle hire 3 km.

**Open:** 1 May - 1 October.

**Directions:** Site is off the Rv 5, 3 km. east of Sogndal, 8 km. west of Kaupanger. GPS: 61.21123, 7.12105

**Charges guide**

| Per unit incl. 2 persons and electricity | NOK 260 |
| --- | --- |
| extra person | NOK 30 |
| child (4-16 yrs) | NOK 10 |

# Andenes Camping

Storgata 53, N-8483 Andenes (Nordland)
t: **76 14 14 12**  e: **camping@whalesafari.no**
alanrogers.com/NO2428  www.andenescamping.no

Accommodation: ☑Pitch ☑Mobile home/chalet ☐ Hotel/B&B ☐ Apartment

Many campsites in Norway have simple and basic facilities with little evidence of security. Often, one arrives, finds a pitch and you pay later when reception opens. Andenes Camping is a classic example, but this extremely popular exposed site at sea level with picturesque mountain backdrop and ocean view, is only three kilometres from the base of 'Whalesafari' and Andenes town. An area of uneven ground provides space for an unspecified number of touring units and you park where you like. The ground is mainly of grass with some hardstanding. Twenty units only can access 16A electricity connections and if you want electricity you are highly advised to arrive by mid-afternoon. 'Whalesafari' is deemed the world's largest, most successful Arctic whale watching operation for the general public. Lying on the west coast of Andøy between the quiet main road (82) and white sandy beaches, the site is also an exceptional location for the midnight sun.

## You might like to know

A wide choice of activities is on offer here – whale, puffin and seal safaris, deep sea fishing trips, great hiking country, kayaking and some great traditional Norwegian food.

☐ Coarse fishing
☐ Fly fishing
☑ Sea fishing
☐ Lake on site
☐ River on site
☐ Lake nearby (max 5 km)
☐ River nearby (max 5 km)
☐ Licence / permit required
☐ Equipment hire available
☐ Bait and fishing supplies

**Facilities:** The reception building houses clean, separate sex sanitary facilities providing for each 2 toilets, 2 showers (10NOK for 5 minutes). with curtain to keep clothes dry and 3 washbasins. In each, one toilet is suitable for disabled visitors and includes a hand basin. Small kitchen with one sink also includes a four ring cooker with oven and two additional hot-plates (free). Motorcaravan service point. Picnic tables. Swings for children. Off site: Well stocked supermarket 250 m. On approach to town a garage, caravan dealer and another supermarket. From the nearby village of Bleik (8 km), trips for deep sea fishing and visits to Bleiksøya one of Norway's most famous bird cliffs to include 80,000 pairs of puffins and 6,000 kittiwakes. Whale safari. Guided walks. Kayaking.

**Open:** 1 June - 30 September.

**Directions:** Travelling north on road 82, site is on the left 3 km. before Andenes.
GPS: 69.29980, 16.05120

### Charges guide

| | |
|---|---|
| Per pitch incl. electricity | NOK 200 |
| tent pitch | NOK 100 |
| car | NOK 100 |

# Trollveggen Camping

Horgheimseidet, N-6300 Åndalsnes (Møre og Romsdal)
t: **71 22 37 00**  e: **post@trollveggen.no**
**alanrogers.com/NO2452  www.trollveggen.no**

Accommodation: ☑Pitch  ☑Mobile home/chalet  ☐ Hotel/B&B  ☐ Apartment

The location of this site provides a unique experience – it is set at the foot of the famous vertical cliff of Trollveggen (the Troll Wall), which is Europe's highest vertical mountain face. The site is pleasantly laid out in terraces with level grass pitches. The facility block, the four cabins and the reception are all very attractively built with grass roofs. Beside the river is an attractive barbecue area where barbecue parties are sometimes arranged. This site is a must for people who love nature. The site is surrounded by the Troll Peaks and the Romsdalshorn Mountains with the rapid river of Rauma flowing by. Here in the beautiful valley of Romsdalen you have the ideal starting point for trips to many outstanding attractions such as 'The Troll Road' to Geiranger or to the Mandalsfossen waterfalls. In the mountains there are nature trails of various lengths and difficulties. The campsite owners are happy to help you with information. The town of Åndalsnes is 10 km. away and has a long tourism tradition as a place to visit. It is situated in the inner part of the beautiful Romsdal fjord and has a range of shops and restaurants.

## You might like to know

Fishing trips in the fjord depart from the quay in Andalsnes. The fishing banks are very close by and Romsdalsfjorden can offer the chance of big fish and a wide variety of species.

- ☐ Coarse fishing
- ☑ Fly fishing
- ☐ Sea fishing
- ☐ Lake on site
- ☐ River on site
- ☐ Lake nearby (max 5 km)
- ☑ River nearby (max 5 km)
- ☑ Licence / permit required
- ☐ Equipment hire available
- ☐ Bait and fishing supplies

**Facilities:** One heated toilet block provides washbasins, some in cubicles, and showers on payment. Family room with baby bath and changing mat, plus facilities for disabled visitors. Communal kitchen with cooking rings, small ovens, fridge and sinks (free hot water). Laundry facilities. Motorcaravan service point. Barbecue area (covered). Playground. Duck pond. Off site: Climbing, glacier walking and hiking. Fjord fishing. Sightseeing trips. The Troll Road. Mardalsfossen (waterfall). Geiranger and Åndalsnes.

**Open:** 10 May - 20 September.

**Directions:** Site is located on the E136 road, 10 km. south of Åndalsnes. It is signed. GPS: 62.49444, 7.758333

**Charges guide**

| Per unit incl. 2 persons and electricity | NOK 190 - 210 |
| --- | --- |
| extra person (over 4 yrs) | NOK 10 |

# Skjerneset Brygge Camping

Ekkilsoya, N-6530 Averøy (Møre og Romsdal)
t: **71 51 18 94**  e: **info@skjerneset.com**
alanrogers.com/NO2490  www.skjerneset.com

**Accommodation:** ☑Pitch  ☑Mobile home/chalet  ☐Hotel/B&B  ☑Apartment

The tiny island of Ekkilsøya lies off the larger island of Averøy and is reached via a side road and bridge from road 64, just south of Bremsnes from where the ferry crosses to Kristiansund. At Skjerneset Camping there is space for 30 caravans or motorcaravans on gravel hardstandings around a rocky bluff and along the harbour's rocky frontage and all have electricity connections. A small grassy area for 5 tents is under pine trees in a hollow on the top of the bluff together with 5 fully equipped cabins. Note: this is a working harbour with deep unfenced water very close to the pitches. Although the fishing industry here is not what it used to be it is still the dominant activity and Skjerneset Camping has been developed by the Otterlei family to give visitors an insight into this industry and its history. The old 'Klippfisk' warehouse is now a fascinating 'fisherimuseum' and also houses the sanitary installations with 5 small apartments, a kitchen, laundry, lounges and reception. The whole site is unique and very charming.

**Facilities:** Unisex sanitary facilities are heated, but basic and include washbasins in cubicles. Two new sanitary blocks. Kitchen. Small laundry. Motorcaravan service point. Kiosk for basic packet foods, crisps, ices, sweets, postcards etc. Satellite TV. Motor boat hire. Organised sea fishing or sightseeing trips in the owner's sea-going boat, and for non anglers who want a fish supper, fresh fish are usually available on site.

**Open:** All year.

**Directions:** Site is on the little island of Ekkilsøya which is reached via a side road running west from the main Rv 64 road, 1.5 km. south of Bremsnes. GPS: 63.08135, 7.59612

**Charges guide**

| Per person | NOK 150 |
| --- | --- |
| pitch | NOK 250 - 500 |
| electricity (10/16A) | NOK 25 |

No credit cards.

## You might like to know

Skjerneset has been the starting point for the family's fish production and fishing boats for almost 100 years. There are still two generations working as fishermen with two fishing boats based at the site.

☐ Coarse fishing
☐ Fly fishing
☑ Sea fishing
☐ Lake on site
☐ River on site
☐ Lake nearby (max 5 km)
☐ River nearby (max 5 km)
☐ Licence / permit required
☑ Equipment hire available
☑ Bait and fishing supplies

# Neset Camping

N-4741 Byglandsfjord (Aust-Agder)
t: **37 93 42 55**  e: **post@neset.no**
alanrogers.com/NO2610  www.neset.no

Accommodation: ☑Pitch  ☑Mobile home/chalet  ☐ Hotel/B&B  ☐ Apartment

On a semi-promontory on the shores of the 40 km. long Byglandsfjord, Neset is a good
centre for activities or as a stop en route north from the ferry port of Kristiansand (from
England or Denmark). Neset is situated on well kept grassy meadows by the lake shore
with the water on three sides and the road on the fourth, and provides 200 unmarked
pitches with electricity and cable TV available. The main building houses reception,
a small shop and a restaurant with fine views over the water. This is a well run, friendly
site where one could spend an active few days. Byglandsfjord offers good fishing
(mainly trout) and the area has marked trails for cycling, riding or walking in an area
famous for its minerals.

## You might like to know

For something different, why not try family
rafting on a specially designed big raft?

☑ Coarse fishing
☐ Fly fishing
☐ Sea fishing
☑ Lake on site
☐ River on site
☐ Lake nearby (max 5 km)
☑ River nearby (max 5 km)
☑ Licence / permit required
☐ Equipment hire available
☐ Bait and fishing supplies

**Facilities:** Three modern sanitary blocks which
can be heated, all with comfortable hot showers
(some on payment), washing up facilities
(metered hot water) and a kitchen. Restaurant
and takeaway (15/6-15/8). Shop (1/5-1/10).
Campers' kitchen. Playground. Lake swimming,
boating and fishing. Excellent new barbecue area
and hot tub. Bicycle, canoe and pedalo hire.
Climbing, rafting and canoeing courses arranged
(including trips to see beavers and elk). Cross-
country skiing possible in winter. Off site: Rock
climbing wall. Marked forest trails.

**Open:** All year.

**Directions:** Site is on route 9, 2.5 km. north of
the town of Byglandsfjord on the eastern shores
of the lake.  GPS: 58.68848, 7.80132

**Charges guide**

| Per person | € 10,00 |
|---|---|
| pitch | € 160,00 |
| child (5-12 yrs) | € 5,00 |
| electricity | € 30,00 |

# Röstånga Camping & Bad

Blinkarpsvägen 3, S-260 24 Röstånga (Skåne Län)
t: 043 591 064  e: nystrand@msn.com
alanrogers.com/SW2630  www.rostangacamping.se

Accommodation: ☑Pitch ☑Mobile home/chalet ☐ Hotel/B&B ☐ Apartment

Beside the Söderåsen National Park, this scenic campsite has its own fishing lake and many activities for the whole family. There are 136 large, level, grassy pitches with electricity (10A) and a quiet area for tents with a view over the fishing lake. The tent area has its own service building and several barbecue places. A large holiday home and 14 pleasant cabins are available to rent all year round. A pool complex adjacent to the site provides a 50 metre swimming pool, three children's pools and a water slide, all heated during peak season. Activities are arranged on the site in high season, including a children's club with exciting activities such as treasure hunts and gold panning, and for adults aqua-aerobics, Nordic walking and tennis. The Söderåsen National Park offers hiking and bicycle trails. The friendly staff will be happy to help you to plan interesting excursions in the area.

## You might like to know
The nearby Söderåsen National Park is known as the 'Grand Canyon' of Skåne. The views through the birch forests along the rim of the canyon are unparalleled in southern Sweden and scientists are continually finding new species of flora and fauna never before seen in the south.

- ☑ Coarse fishing
- ☐ Fly fishing
- ☐ Sea fishing
- ☑ Lake on site
- ☐ River on site
- ☐ Lake nearby (max 5 km)
- ☐ River nearby (max 5 km)
- ☐ Licence / permit required
- ☐ Equipment hire available
- ☐ Bait and fishing supplies

**Facilities:** Four good, heated sanitary blocks with free hot water and facilities for babies and disabled visitors. Laundry with washing machines and dryers. Kitchen with cooking rings, oven and microwave. Motorcaravan service point. Small shop at reception. Bar, restaurant and takeaway. Minigolf. Tennis. Fitness trail. Fishing. Canoe hire. Children's club. WiFi. Off site: Swimming pool complex adjacent to site (free for campers as is a visit to the Zoo). Many golf courses nearby. Motor racing track at Ring Knutstorp 8 km.

**Open:** 9 April - 18 October.

**Directions:** From Malmö: drive towards Lund and follow road no. 108 to Röstånga. From Stockholm: turn off at Østra Ljungby and take road no. 13 to Röstånga. In Röstånga drive through the village on road no. 108 and follow the signs. GPS: 55.996583, 13.28005

**Charges guide**

| | |
|---|---|
| Per unit incl. 2 persons and electricity | SEK 200 - 295 |

# Hafsten Swecamp Resort

Hafsten 120, S-451 96 Uddevalla (Västra Götalands Län)
t: 052 264 4117   e: info@hafsten.se
alanrogers.com/SW2725   www.hafsten.se

Accommodation: ☑Pitch ☑Mobile home/chalet ☐ Hotel/B&B ☐ Apartment

This privately owned site on the west coast is situated on a peninsula overlooking the magnificent coastline of Bohuslän. Open all year, it is a lovely terraced site with a beautiful, shallow and child-friendly sandy beach and many nature trails in the vicinity. There are 180 touring pitches, all with electricity (10A), 70 of them with water and drainage. In all, there are 330 pitches including a tent area and 60 cottages of a high standard. There are plenty of activities available including, canoeing, fishing, horse riding, minigolf, tennis, clay pigeon shooting, water slide and a paddling pool (charged), boat and motor boat hire. Troubadour evenings are arranged during the summer. Almost any activity can be arranged on the site or elsewhere by the friendly owners if they are given advance notice. Amenities include two clean and well maintained service buildings, a pub, a fully licensed restaurant with wine from their own French vineyard, and a well stocked shop (all open all year) and a takeaway (1/6-31/8).

## You might like to know

Fishing for cod and whiting is also possible in the fjord.

☑ Coarse fishing
☐ Fly fishing
☐ Sea fishing
☑ Lake on site
☐ River on site
☐ Lake nearby (max 5 km)
☐ River nearby (max 5 km)
☑ Licence / permit required
☐ Equipment hire available
☐ Bait and fishing supplies

**Facilities:** Two heated sanitary buildings provide the usual facilities. Showers are on payment. Kitchen with good cooking facilities and dishwashing sinks. Dining room. Laundry facilities. Units for disabled visitors. Motorcaravan services. Shop. Restaurant, takeaway and pub. Troubadour evenings. TV room. Relaxation centre with sauna and jacuzzi (charged). Water slide (charged). Internet access (WiFi). Riding. Minigolf. Tennis. Playground. Off site: Nordens Ark (animal park) 40 km. Havets hus (marine museum) 30 km. Golf 13 km. Shopping centre 13 km.

**Open:** All year.

**Directions:** From the E6, north Uddevalla, at Torpmotet exit take the 161 road towards Lysekil. At the Rotviksbro roundabout take the 161 road towards Orust. The exit to the site is located further on road 2 km. on the left. Follow the signs for 4 km. It is a narrow, one way road for motorcaravans and caravans.
GPS: 58.314683, 11.723333

**Charges guide**

| | |
|---|---|
| Per pitch incl. electricity | SEK 210 - 330 |

# Camping Haapasaaren Lomakylä

Haapasaarentie 5, FIN-34600 Ruovesi (Häme)
t: **044 080 0290**  e: **lomakyla@haapasaari.fi**
alanrogers.com/FI2840  www.ruovedenhaapasaarenmatkailu.fi

**Accommodation:** ☑Pitch  ☑Mobile home/chalet  ☐ Hotel/B&B  ☐ Apartment

Haapasaaren is located on Lake Näsijärvi, around 70 km. north of Tampere in south western Finland. This is a well equipped site with a café and restaurant, a traditional Finnish outside dancing area and, of course, plenty of saunas! Rowing boats, canoes, cycles and, during the winter months, sleds are all available for rent. Fishing is very popular here. Pitches are grassy and of a good size. There is also a good range of accommodation to rent, including holiday cottages with saunas. The cosy restaurant, Jätkäinkämppä, has an attractive terrace and fine views across the lake. Haapasaaren's friendly owners organize a series of guided tours throughout the year. These include hiking and nature treks, berry and mushroom picking, and, during the winter, ice fishing and cross-country skiing. Helvetinjärvi National Park is one of the most dramatic areas of western Finland, and is made up of deep gorges and dense forests. There is a rich population of birds and occasionally even brown bears and lynx can be seen here.

**Facilities:** Café. Restaurant. Direct lake access. Saunas. Fishing. Minigolf. Boat and canoe hire. Bicycle hire. Guided tours. Play area. Tourist information. Chalets for rent. Off site: Walking and cycle routes. Boat trips. Helvetinjärvi National Park.

**Open:** All year.

**Directions:** From Helsinki, head north on the E12 motorway to Tampere and then northeast on N63-9 to Orivesi. Then, continue north on road 66 to Ruovesi and follow signs to the site. GPS: 61.99413, 24.069843

**Charges guide**

| Per unit incl. 2 persons and electricity | € 25,00 |
|---|---|
| extra person | € 4,00 |
| child (under 15 yrs) | € 2,00 |

## Special offers
Special discounts in May and October and a traditional Finnish smoke sauna one evening. Night fishing option in August and September. Winter fishing trips.

## You might like to know
Special fishing trips organised by the site, particularly an ice fishing and burbot catching trip.

☐ Coarse fishing
☐ Fly fishing
☑ Sea fishing
☐ Lake on site
☐ River on site
☑ Lake nearby (max 5 km)
☐ River nearby (max 5 km)
☐ Licence / permit required
☐ Equipment hire available
☐ Bait and fishing supplies

# Camping Lakari

Lakarintie 405, FIN-34800 Virrat (Häme)
t: **034 758 639**  e: **lakari@virtainmatkailu.fi**
alanrogers.com/FI2830  www.virtainmatkailu.fi

Accommodation: ☑Pitch  ☑Mobile home/chalet  ☐ Hotel/B&B  ☐ Apartment

The peace and tranquillity of the beautiful natural surroundings are the main attractions at this vast (18 hectares) campsite which is located on a narrow piece of land between two lakes. This site is a must if you want to get away from it all. There is a variety of cabins to rent, some with their own beach and jetty! Marked pitches for tents and caravans are beside the beach or in little meadows in the forest. You pick your own place. Site amenities include a café and a beach sauna. This is a spectacular landscape with deep gorges and steep lakeside cliffs. A nature trail from the site leads to the lakes of Toriseva or pleasant excursions to the Esteri Zoo and the village shop in Keskinen. The Helvetinjärvi National Park is nearby. Facilities at the site are rather basic but very clean and well kept. This is a glorious place for a nature loving tourist looking to relax.

## You might like to know

A nature trail leads to the Toriseva gorge lakes. The Pirkan Taival hiking trail passes through the campsite. Fishing grounds within easy reach include the Herraskoski and Kotalan Kosket Rapids.

☑ **Coarse fishing**
☐ **Fly fishing**
☐ **Sea fishing**
☑ **Lake on site**
☐ **River on site**
☐ **Lake nearby (max 5 km)**
☑ **River nearby (max 5 km)**
☑ **Licence / permit required**
☐ **Equipment hire available**
☐ **Bait and fishing supplies**

**Facilities:** Two toilet blocks, basic but clean and well kept include toilets, washbasins and showers. Free hot water. Chemical disposal and motorcaravan service point. Covered campers' kitchen with fridge, cooking rings and oven. Washing machine. Small shop and cafeteria. TV. Fishing. Bicycle hire. Off site: Golf 1 km. Riding 5 km.

**Open:** 1 May - 30 September.

**Directions:** Site is 7 km. south of Virrat on road 66. Follow signs. GPS: 62.209817, 23.837767

### Charges guide

| Per unit incl. 2 persons | |
|---|---|
| and electricity | € 22,00 |
| extra person | € 3,00 |
| child | € 1,50 |

# Ukonjärvi Camping

Ukonjärventi 141, FIN-99801 Ivalo (Lapland)
t: **016 667 501**  e: **nuttu@ukolo.fi**
alanrogers.com/FI2995  www.ukolo.fi

**Accommodation:** ☑Pitch ☑Mobile home/chalet ☐ Hotel/B&B ☐ Apartment

Ukonjärvi Camping lies on the banks of Lake Inari, situated in a forested area alongside a nature reserve. It is a quiet, peaceful site, ideal for rest and relaxation. Thirty touring pitches have electricity and are surrounded by pine and beech trees. Cottages are available to rent. A bar and restaurant are located at reception; a range of local dishes are produced including reindeer casserole. There is also a barbecue hut, located in the centre of the site, if you prefer to cook your own food. A climb up to the nearby viewpoint offers spectacular views over the lake – you can even see over to Russia. The lake also provides plenty of opportunities for boating and fishing.

## You might like to know
The vast Lake Inari covers 1,040 m². There are over 3,000 islands in total. Trout, lake, salmon, white fish, perch and pike are all found in Lake Inaris' waters.

☑ Coarse fishing
☐ Fly fishing
☐ Sea fishing
☑ Lake on site
☐ River on site
☐ Lake nearby (max 5 km)
☑ River nearby (max 5 km)
☑ Licence / permit required
☐ Equipment hire available
☐ Bait and fishing supplies

**Facilities:** Sanitary block includes toilets and showers. Laundry and campers' kitchen. Lakeside sauna (extra cost). Bar and restaurant. Barbecue hut with logs. Small beach. Fishing and boating on lake. TV room. WiFi. Off site: Tankavaaran Kansainvalinen Kulamuseo, a gold mining experience where you can try gold panning, keeping what you find! The Northern Lapland Centre and the Sami Museum, displaying cultural and natural history exhibitions.

**Open:** May - September.

**Directions:** Ukonjärvi Camping is 11 km. north of Ivalo on route 4. Look for signs to Lake Inari viewpoint; site is about 1 km. down the narrow road (signed). GPS: 68.73687, 27.47687

**Charges guide**

| | |
|---|---|
| Per person | € 3,50 |
| child | € 2,50 |
| pitch incl. electricity | € 19,00 |

# Been to any good campsites lately?
## We have

You'll find them here...

The UK's market leading independent guides to the best campsites

...and, new for 2011, here...

101 great campsites, ideal for your specific hobby, pastime or passion

# Want independent campsite reviews at your fingertips?

You'll find them here...

Over 3,000 in-depth campsite reviews at **www.alanrogers.com**

alan
rogers

...and even here...

An exciting free app from iTunes and the Apple app store*

*available January 2011

# Want to book your holiday on one of Europe's top campsites?

We can do it for you. No problem.

The best campsites in the most popular regions - we'll take care of everything

alan rogers ⦸ travel

alan rogers

Discover the best campsites in Europe
with Alan Rogers

**alanrogers.com**
01580 214000

# index

# index

# index